scm centrebooks · christian casebooks

already published
Managing the Church / *W. E. Beveridge*
The Casework Ministry / *Joan B. Miller*
Case Studies in Unity / *R. M. C. Jeffery*

in preparation
The Christian in Education / *Colin Alves*
An Eye for an Ear / *Trevor Beeson*
Solitary Refinement / *Sister Madeleine* OSA

R. M. C. Jeffery

Case Studies in Unity

SCM PRESS LTD

334 00161 7

First published 1972
by SCM Press Ltd
56 Bloomsbury Street London

© *SCM Press Ltd 1972*

Printed in Great Britain by
Richard Clay (*The Chaucer Press*) *Ltd*
Bungay, Suffolk

Contents

	Prologue	7
1	Some Models	9
2	Finding New Life	26
3	PND and All That	45
4	Local Councils of Churches	61
5	The Ecumenical Parish	77
6	Planning for Mission	94
7	The Emerging Church	110
	Epilogue	128

Acknowledgments

This book could not have been written without the help and assistance of many people who have much greater local experience than I. Special thanks are due to John Oxborough, the Rev. Ivor Smith-Cameron, the Rev. John Hammersley, the Rev. Norman James, the Rev. Barrie Hinksman, the Rev. Frank Scuffham, the Rev. Derek Jones, the Rev. Dick Jones, the Rev. Hugo de Waal and the Bishop of Stepney. Parts of chapters 5 and 7 were originally delivered as the Lovell Murray Memorial Lectures at the Ecumenical Institute of Canada in February 1971. I am grateful to the Director of the Institute, Canon Puxley, for his help and hospitality on that occasion. Part of chapter 3 was originally a paper prepared for the World Council of Churches and part of chapter 6 appeared as an article in the Cowley Fathers' magazine *New Fire* in 1970. I am grateful to Fr C. R. Bryant SSJE for permission to use it here.

I am extremely grateful to Ruth, my wife, who has not only put up with my doing extra work to write this book but has also typed the final manuscript.

R. M. C. JEFFERY

Prologue

Ever since the Acts of the Apostles the life of the church has been told in stories of what people have done in response to the gospel. This book tells some very undramatic stories of the way in which the church is being made and remade by Christians today.

They are stories about the search for unity. Unity is not easy to find or to keep. It is a dynamic thing, and unless new stories are for ever being told, unless people are for ever making the church for themselves, that unity will never be found. There is little that is new in this book. The SCM Press in 1941 published a book by Hugh Martin entitled *Christian Reunion*. Our progress has been so slow that much that he wrote then still holds true today. This shows us how important it is to keep to our ecumenical vision today. It is not easy to do so, but a few stories may help.

1 Some Models

I

On the night of 15 April 1912 the passenger liner *Titanic* sank after hitting an iceberg while crossing the Atlantic Ocean. About a third of the passengers were saved, mainly as a result of the heroism of John Phillips, the wireless operator, who sent out signals which enabled a nearby ship to come to the rescue. Phillips, with a lifebelt strapped to his body, continued at his post until the wireless room was flooded. When he finally struggled up on deck he was washed overboard by a wave and never seen again.

Phillips had been a choirboy at Farncombe parish church in his youth and in this investigation of local ecumenism it is to Farncombe and Godalming that we first turn. At a time when many feel as if ecumenism is sinking fast under the waves, the Godalming Council of Churches is one of a few places where local unity seems to be effectively emerging. Perhaps like Phillips even Godalming will finally be swept away, but at the time of writing there is no sign of this.

Godalming in Surrey has a present population of 17,000. It is mainly a commuter town for London and is five miles from Guildford. The town itself has a long history going back to Saxon times and was at one time, before the reformation, a place of pilgrimage. In the seventeenth century there developed a strong tradition of independency in the church. This was in part due to the parish priest of Godalming, who disliked preaching. He is reported to have said that

> . . . the surfeit of the word is of all most dangerous and the silliest creatures have longest ears, and the preaching was the worst part of God's worship, and that if he left out anything, he would leave out that.

This may well have been said in response to the accusations brought against him by some of his parishioners who complained that he was

> a haunter and frequenter of tippling inns and taverns and used gaming both at cards and at table as well upon the Lord's day as others.

He was certainly not popular, and this may well have been one of the reasons why the Victoria County History reports that by 1669 Godalming had become 'very largely nonconformist'.

There was also an attack on the established church from the followers of George Fox, who formed a small society in 1655. One of these, Henry Gill, in 1658 wrote a pamphlet entitled *Warning and Visitation to the Inhabitants of Godalming*. This began with the words:

> All ye inhabitants of Godalming which have any desire after the Lord, read this paper with moderation, and I shall show you how you are deceived by him you call your minister.

Gill and others also refused to pay their tithes to the vicar and were imprisoned for it and continued to oppose him so that some of them

> for opposition to the priest . . . at Godalming were much beaten and abused, and put into the cage there.[1]

By 1669, the vicar of Godalming reported that there were two conventicles in the town. These were a weekly congregation of Presbyterians and a monthly gathering of Quakers. He estimated their numbers to be between 400 and 500 each, and he did not know who their teachers were. By 1689 the Friends had a meeting house; a Presbyterian meeting house had been established in 1672. We learn that there were between 1,200 and 1,500 independents in the town by 1689.

In 1797 a Methodist chapel was established. During the nineteenth century further Anglican churches were built including the one in Farncombe, and a Baptist chapel was built in 1903.

Today Godalming Christians no longer live in great fear or in mutual hostility. Rather through the Godalming and District Council of Churches a pattern of church co-operation is emerging in which there is very strong lay initiative and the independency of old is being followed by creative corporate action.

How has this come about and what is going on? The people in Godalming would be the first to admit that they were very fortunate to reach a point of ecumenical growth where all things came together for good at exactly the right psychological moment. The council of churches was formed in 1959. It started at a time when many other local councils began, but before the great rush of councils which came in the mid-1960s. For the first few years the council of churches did the kind of things which most of them do, such as observance of the Week of Prayer for Christian Unity, a Good Friday procession, annual carol services. There was little formal organization and people came together just to do these things rather than because a committee had been set up with specific responsibilities.

In 1967 the council of churches decided to take part in the People Next Door programme which had been centrally sponsored by the British Council of Churches and the Conference of British Missionary Societies. They delayed the start of the programme until the autumn (the majority of places took the Week of Prayer for Christian Unity as their starting point) but organized it very efficiently. A small group gave it their priority, and one person put great effort

11

into setting it up, spending hours on the telephone and in making personal contact with people to get them to take part. He and others saw the programme as a real opportunity for the 'man in the pew' to say what kind of church he wanted and to attempt to move things on a bit at every level. The fact that there was a two-way flow of information and that people could for once make their opinions heard at the level of the national churches was a great attraction. The programme began with a public meeting of about 150 people, who then for five weeks met in groups of ten in each other's houses. The whole group met finally amidst a great burst of enthusiasm and out of this came an eight-page report of recommendations, which was circulated to 1,500 people. These findings were not very startling. Many other PND groups came up with very similar lists of recommendations.[2] The difference about the Godalming situation was that people were prepared to act on them.

Some people thought that PND was going to take over the role of the council of churches and become an independent organization. So it was the council of churches which set up six sub-committees to deal with the recommendations. These were (a) worship, study and prayer, (b) publicity, (c) welfare, (d) social responsibility, (e) Christian Aid, (f) education. In so many places this was as far as things went. Not so in Godalming; this was the beginning of considerable lay initiative and action.

What has been going on? One very notable feature has been the preparation by the people themselves of study material for use in groups. The first course was 'God speaks to Godalming through the Bible', and this ended with a fellowship meal on Maundy Thursday which was attended by over 100 people. The next year a course was arranged on 'Prayer is my job'. This centred on the nature of prayer and one of the results of this course was a very imaginative programme for the Week of Prayer for Christian Unity which allowed for a variety of patterns of prayer and worship. This was followed by a course entitled 'World need – Christian Action' which centred on the concerns for world development and led to the establishment of a local Action for World Development Group. All these programmes, which took place during the winter months, usually before Christmas, beginning with PND in the autumn of 1967, had been based on a similar pattern – an initial public meeting with a speaker, followed by a series of meetings in ecumenical house groups and a final meeting to assess the findings. In 1970 this pattern was altered. The organizers became aware that by acting in this way they were 'creaming off' the ecumenically minded and not doing much for the average churchgoer. So they devised a much more ambitious course on the Holy Spirit entitled 'The Wind of Change'. This tied in with the theme of the Week of Prayer for Christian Unity. It was devised in three parts so that people could opt for different aspects of the subject. Also, apart from the opening and closing sessions, the course was designed for use within the congregations rather than by ecumenical groups. Thus many more people were involved.

The welfare committee has organized a system of road stewards and a good neighbour scheme. This has not always worked and needs very careful servicing. The committee has also produced a directory of all the social facilities in Godalming. If this work continues to grow there may be a need for a paid organizer in the social welfare field. This was suggested in the PND report. One council of churches at Corby in Northamptonshire does have a full-time social worker, and her salary and expenses are paid by the local authorities. The Christian Aid committee concentrates its work on Christian Aid Week, where the amount of money raised has gone up from £1,300 to £2,500 in three years.

13

This is efficiently organized and is based on a specific project to which people can give real attention and which gets considerable publicity in the local press. The other committees on social responsibility and education have been less active. But the social responsibility committee arranged a teach-in on the Nigeria/Biafra situation and issued a statement afterwards. The education committee is investigating the problem of religious education in schools and a youth committee is trying to co-ordinate the work of the various church youth organizations. Other activities which the council of churches organizes are an annual carol service and youth services using experimental forms of worship.

Many councils of churches would find most of this more than enough but it is not all. A vital part of this exercise lies in the communications and publicity network which has been established in Godalming. One part of this is an energetic and efficient publicity officer who began by organizing PND. His basic approach is a personal one. A great deal of time is spent on the telephone and in personally delivering material to people. This is backed up by printed leaflets and posters, etc., but he is convinced that personal contact is essential. Also the local press, again through personal contact, is kept fully briefed on activities and is therefore pleased to provide a considerable amount of news in the local paper.

Then there is *Link*. This is the magazine of the Godalming council of Churches. This was another direct result of the People Next Door programme and the operation is best described by the editor:

> ... after a fairly hurried discussion a meeting of those concerned with existing church magazines was held, about twenty attending. Half a dozen of these were professionally competent in the fields of writing and publishing and these drew up a proposal for a magazine 'of which the major part would be common to local member churches but with an inner core peculiar to each church. Its aim would be to

provide a local platform for Christian news views and opinions on the great religious issues of the day.' By means of many personal approaches and much lobbying enough churches agreed to make a go-ahead possible and we stuck our necks out and said we'd be in print on Palm Sunday 1969 – nine months after the idea was first considered. *Link*, as it is called, now circulates 3,100 copies a month to 13 churches and what we think is its unique feature is that in the case of four churches it replaces their existing magazines; they just produce an inset. Whilst we hope others will follow suit at the moment they use *Link* as an inset to their own magazine, or use it in parallel or just take some copies. Each church's news of more general interest is included in a 'round the churches' item in *Link*, which mainly consists of articles *all* written by local people, mainly lay, on subjects such as school assemblies, pre-marital sex, praying with children, underdeveloped countries and a series on 'People and Books that have Influenced me'.[3]

Link is produced by an independent editorial board. Its financial basis lies in nine pages of advertising which brings in a revenue of £900 per annum and enables copies to be sold to the churches for 1½p each so that the churches can sell it to their members at 2½p. It is a glossy, well-produced magazine, and if it has a tendency to be rather pious that is because people like it that way. It has become a forum for the exchange of ideas and complaints, though it should be said that 85 per cent of its circulation is through the Anglican churches, since they are the dominant denomination in the town.

Godalming certainly has people with business acumen. The council of churches itself is financed by contributions of £10 per annum from the larger churches and £5 from the smaller ones. This enables them to cover all their expenses. Most councils of churches in this country are lucky to receive £1 from their member churches, let alone £5 or £10!

What is the role of the clergy in all this? This is rather difficult to assess. They certainly take a back seat in terms of organization. Nearly all the activities are lay-initiated and

15

lay-led. Certainly the clergy give support to the council of churches and this is a great help. Some may well feel a little anxious about all the ecumenical work. One has recently written in his parish notes that while all this ecumenism is all right, people must remember that their main function is to worship in his church on Sunday. He is obviously feeling a little threatened. At the same time no attempt has been made through the council of churches to question independent congregational life in Godalming. There is plenty of variety there still. Nevertheless, the laity seem to have achieved a freedom which is not so obvious in many other places. When asked about the clergy one of the leading lights of the council replied, 'It all depends how you handle them!' Not many laity have this healthy attitude to the clergy. When the diocesan Bishop came to open one of the autumn study programmes his style did not appeal to some of the lay people of Godalming. They were not afraid to say so and the next number of *Link* contained several letters complaining about the bishop's flippant manner. Whether the complaints were justified or not is not our concern; the fact is that people felt they had the freedom to say these things and *Link* had the freedom to publish them. They also published a moderating letter from one of the clergy in the next issue. It is as if the independent attitude which we saw in seventeenth-century Godalming has somehow survived or been revived, this time not in a spirit of sectarianism but in a spirit of ecumenism and Christian freedom.

Another factor in Godalming is the presence of the Farncombe Community. This ecumenical women's community founded in 1963 has given quiet support to ecumenism in Godalming. It has also provided a centre of prayer at the heart of the place and this may be more significant than we can ever know. At the time of writing there is also a hippy commune in Godalming, and another more informal attempt

16

to establish a rather Pentecostal type of Christian community. There is also a Roman Catholic convent.

Godalming is not unique. It is not a great success story. It owes a very great deal to its sociological setting and to the type of middle-class, energetic, articulate London commuter who lives there. It is a small enough town to have a sense of community. Moreover it may fairly be asked what would happen if five or six key people left or if the clergy were less co-operative. There have certainly been difficulties. The Baptist church opted out at a very early stage. Godalming does not show us a blue-print for others to follow. What it shows us is what can happen if a few people discover that they have the freedom to act in new ways and find the right means of communicating this to others.

Perhaps the secret lies in these words from the editor of *Link*:

> . . . there has been a degree of spontaneity, of readiness to take a risk, some real openness to the winds of the Spirit rather than the counsels of prudence. Not much, but enough to get us just a few inches above the ground of denomination and towards the free air of the spirit of loving community.[4]

This presumably is what the gospel is all about and in this way Godalming is sending out a message about what it means to be the church and a Christian today.

II

Students at the Imperial College of Science and Queen Elizabeth College, in South Kensington, have over the last few years found themselves faced with a new kind of church. This has come about as the result of many years of hard work and experimenting by the Anglican Chaplains, Ivor Smith-Cameron and Ron Diss. The Chaplaincy has no church – it used to share one of the local churches but this is no longer thought necessary. Sunday worship takes place in one of the college lounges. It is an informal and spontaneous, though never a casual affair, including scripture readings and communion. People are often invited during the service to talk about their week-day work in other places. People receive communion standing where they are. The service is very ecumenical – no questions are asked about denominational differences. It is just a group of Christians worshipping together. 'Filling people, not pews!'

During the week, all around the colleges, in halls of residence, in laboratories, in student study bedrooms and in lecture theatres, small groups gather for study and for discussion, for the breaking of bread and the opening up of the Word. There are now about thirty-five such group meetings each week. Perhaps half of them will be set within the context of the Eucharist, while others are groups for prayer, reflection or service to the community. Over 350 people receive communion each week. The chaplaincy is based on the principle of worship being the point from which service and evangelism will spring, yet the worship is not rigid and stereotyped but emerges out of the actual life of the groups. Here, then, is a living Christian community which in this context of science has already produced twenty-one priests with another three in training at the moment.

Here are Christians exercising freedom and also simply accepting each other as Christians. Underlying this approach is a strong emphasis on personal contact and a strong conviction that the mission of the church is not confined in any way to buildings but is concerned with the encounter with people. The chaplaincy aims to lift people from dependent relationships to freedom and responsibility, and if there are going to do this they must express this freedom and flexibility themselves.

There is here an awareness that the use of the small group is an essential part of the way in which the church will work in the world today. This has been very carefully examined by John Taylor in his CMS Newsletters, some of which were subsequently issued as a pamphlet entitled *Breaking Down the Parish*.

> Vociferously it is asserted that the parish system is breaking down; unhappily too many parish priests are, all over the world. My plea is that deliberately and confidently we should allow the parishes to break down into those smaller, more spontaneous units of Christian presence which our mobile, cosmopolitan, New Testament kind of world demands.[5]

It was Ernest Southcott at Halton, Leeds, who established a parish based mainly upon the house church. This was considered very forward-looking at the time and regarded with much suspicion. The use of house groups for parish or ecumenical work is now a normal part of the life of the church in many areas. This developed out of the People Next Door programme at Godalming, and in other places. The use of groups in another form is one of the keynotes of the work of urban and industrial mission on Tees-side.

After many years of growing industrial mission on Tees-side the churches there, through the council of churches, are developing a pattern of urban mission to the whole area. The plan for their work, *Structuring the Church for Mission*,[6] is now widely known and provides very useful material for other areas wishing to look at the mission of the church in terms of the whole of society. The strength of Tees-side is a group of people who are working hard to put these proposals into practice. While there are still many difficulties ahead the churches are acknowledging the value of what is being attempted and giving it support. The report proposes a strategy for mission with the following pattern of ministry:

1. *Local neighbourhood ministries.* This is the role of the parish ministry in relation to home and family life. They see this developing through ecumenical co-operation and sharing. However they also

think it is unfortunate that out of 175 clergy in Tees-side as many as 160 work in this ministry only.

2. *Crisis ministries.* In this area lies the concern for co-operation with the social services, downtown and twilight areas, vagrancy and similar problems.

3. *The civic level.* Here they are concerned for relationships with local government, political parties, education, the law, the police and the planning authorities.

4. *Industry and commerce.* This continues the work of industrial mission, work in the technical college and concern for commerce, and the leisure industry.

To back all this up, they are working towards the establishment of a research and training unit which will provide not only information but theological insights for the whole area, and involve the training of the people of God to play their proper role in society. One of the basic tools used in this approach is that of the 'frontier group'. By this is meant the bringing together of Christians and non-Christians to explore common concerns and to exchange ideas and presuppositions. The frontier group is a form of mission and a way of doing theology. Theology comes alive out of the encounter of the gospel with the world and the frontier group provides a way of enabling this to happen. The theologian is often a useful person in such a group as an interpreter, who can help lay people do theology for themselves. In this way people become articulate about the implications of Christianity for themselves and their work. Thus theology becomes a reality and has a missionary dimension. It also forces the theologian to rethink and reinterpret his own theology.

One of the great values of the Tees-side approach is that it shows us how the work of the church must take seriously the structures of society. Each level of society requires a different approach and we thus see how diverse the ministry of the church must be. For far too long the church has assumed that there was only one pattern of mission, that to the residential aspect of society. Also as soon as the church begins to move outside this area ecumenism becomes a necessity, not a luxury.

III

Two other illustrations of the non-parochial approach to society are seen in the work of the Yorkshire Churches Group and of Scottish Churches House, Dunblane.

The Yorkshire Churches Group came into existence under the auspices of the Yorkshire Council of Social Service. This group was able to make response on behalf of the churches to the Regional Economic Planning Report, and so enter into dialogue with the planning authority on matters relating to the region. Their report *The Churches and Regionalism* defines the areas of particular concern to the churches and justifies the churches' involvement in the following terms:

> We believe all life is the concern of God; that he is at work in history; that therefore the Christian church must be concerned with all aspects of life and that it is false distinction between personal and social religion which robs Christianity of its relevance. Certainly man's dignity is obscured by unworthy social and physical conditions and his resentment aroused by inequality of opportunity. If the Christian church is insensitive to this she cannot uphold with any consistency the dignity of men as children of God.[7]

The report has enabled the churches to participate more fully in campaigns to prevent pollution and has given them an understanding of many social problems. The group continues to review new developments and has been able to help the churches and councils of churches to understand the significance for them of other recent reports like the Seebohm and the Hunt reports. In spite of the significance of this work the group has so far failed to gain sufficient financial backing from the ecclesiastical authorities in the area to enable the work to be developed further.

Scottish Churches House, Dunblane, was opened in 1961 under the auspices of most of the churches in Scotland. There had been several years of planning before that which had been inspired by two notable Scottish ecumenical figures, Archie Craig and Robert Mackie. They saw the house as having a very open function, providing a centre with a devotional life around which much of the work would be self-programmed. They saw the house existing to 'serve the whole church for the whole of its task' and also to 'help people to pray in the circumstances of the present-day world'. The house, under the leadership of Ian Fraser, rapidly became a meeting place for all sorts of people. It was a centre for retreats, for inter-church discussion, for work with apprentices, for high-powered debate on social, political and moral questions in Scotland. Many new enterprises have been launched from the house, but above all it is a place where many lay people come to learn to 'do theology' in a new and living way. Ian Fraser has emphasized that the house had to be a place for creative listening both to the people who came and also to the events of the world, so that Christians could discover their proper response to them. The house is a place of common learning and therefore a place of evangelism. Ian Fraser has summed it up as follows:

Such a centre can help to equip God's people for their work of ministry. This will be a work of mutual upbuilding in which church members share what they have and receive from others . . . The theological insights of those who work in theological colleges drawing their material mainly from books and of those who seek to serve God in the workaday world, will correct, challenge, confirm one another. The word 'training' does not fit very well the assistance in growth towards maturity which requires everyone to contribute and everyone to receive. The word 'formation' may have to be brought into more general currency, since it suggests both the shaping up of life which can come from a power outside man's own efforts, and contributions from many quarters. Scottish Churches House could also be called a centre for formation. It exists to offer the church humble service at points where the whole people of God may be more effectively equipped for their work of ministry, in worship, in theology, in service and in proclamation.[8]

So through its courses, conferences and retreats Scottish Churches House enables Christians together to gain a new understanding of their faith and to find new ways of communicating and expressing it to others.

IV

Just outside Cambridge there is a new private housing estate called Barhill. The houses are not particularly attractive, the area is rather bleak and it must be rather cold when the winds blow. When the estate was being planned the churches in Cambridge, Anglican and Free Church, came together to discuss what they should do about pastoral provision for Barhill. They agreed to tackle the project ecumenically. The Anglicans nominated the vicar in whose parish Barhill lay to be responsible from the Anglican end and the Free Churches found a retired Congregational minister who was willing to live and work in Barhill. He was provided with a house for the purpose. The area has been designated one of ecumenical experiment. Most of the church work takes place in house groups and study groups. The community centre is sometimes used for worship, when the Holy Communion is celebrated and intercommunion practised. The project is already growing and changing. A new Free Church minister is now there and plans are well advanced for a church building. Here the membership of the church is growing in numbers and people are coming into contact with the Christian community for the first time. Those who describe themselves as 'weary of denominationalism' also find Barhill an attractive place to live in for this reason.

Barhill is one of thirty such areas of ecumenical experiment in Britain.

V

These are some models of what local unity is about and what local unity is becoming in Britain today. These illustrations provide a basis for a deeper examination of local unity. It would be wrong to generalize from these models. Those involved in them would not regard them as particularly exceptional and other people would be able to give similar illustrations from their own experience. These models may begin to give us a few clues about the shape of the church which is emerging today. It would seem that lay initiative is an important factor and that people should feel free to take risks and make experiments. The use of the small group is in many ways a necessary means of learning and sharing. Experiments in patterns of worship are needed. At the same time people have to learn to do theology for themselves and to do it in terms of the whole of life and not just their own personal situation. The church's missionary strategy needs to be related to all levels of society and not limited to the personal level. Even though some think that the institutional church is sinking irrevocably below the waves of secularism, there are at least signs of hope, and the signals which will mean a new beginning and a new life are sounding out pretty strongly from some places.

NOTES

1. I am grateful to Mr John Oxborough of Godalming for providing me with this historical information together with other material on the Godalming Council of Churches.

2. See C. K. Sansbury and others *Agenda for the Churches*, SCM Press 1967, for an overall picture of the findings of PND.

3. Roy Farrant, 'Godalming Council of Churches', *New Directions*, New Series Vol. 1 No. 3, 1969, pp.43–6.

4. *Ibid.*

5. J. V. Taylor, *Breaking Down the Parish*, CMS 1968, p.5.

6. B. Cooper and others, *Structuring the Church for Mission*, Bolton, 1968.

7. *The Churches and Regionalism*, Yorkshire Council for Social Service 1969.

8. I. M. Fraser, *People Journeying*, Scottish Churches House 1969, p.208.

2 Finding New Life

I

There must be at least 10,000 people in this country who are keenly interested in the cause of Christian unity. A large number of them are unconnected with any movement or organization working directly or indirectly for it. Most of them are ordinary loyal, but perhaps critical, members of their local churches.

This was the assumption and the plea for members which appeared on the back page of the first number of the Bulletin of the Friends of Reunion in 1934. It is an assumption that today many people would be unwilling to make. It is very difficult to find out what the 'man in the pew' thinks about unity. It is even more difficult to persuade him to join a campaign. Campaigning is normally a minority activity, but it is a significant one which can effectively change the direction of institutions and the attitudes of people.

The Friends of Reunion is an interesting example of such a pressure group. It never obtained the amount of support which it would have liked, but during the 1930s and to a lesser extent the 1950s it was an effective body in pressing the need for unity (both organic and local) and also for intercommunion. Those who formed it were a group of very significant people on the ecclesiastical scene of the time. The first secretaries were S. C. Carpenter, then Dean of Exeter, and Hugh Martin, the leading Baptist ecumenist. The first chairman was Mervyn Haigh, the highly influential Anglican Bishop of Coventry. The Friends aimed to arrange public meetings and lectures all over the country. They issued a bulletin which provided news about union movements all over the world. They held an annual conference in which key issues were discussed and behind the scenes they worked hard to pressurize the key people. They also issued a series of publications to promote understanding of ecumenical matters. They were able to use some of the most able minds of the church for many of their activities. In their early years they were greatly concerned to promote understanding and support for the Church of South India, the scheme for which was being negotiated at that time. They also produced a draft scheme for a united church in England which is still worth studying. At the same time they were trying to increase their membership and stimulate their own members to local action. One member described in the bulletin what his own intentions were:

1. I will try never to speak slightingly or disparagingly of any Christian denomination.
2. I will try to look out for and embrace whatever opportunities may present themselves of co-operating in good works with the members of other denominations so far as this can be done without disloyalty to my own.
3. I will support to the best of my ability whatever inter-church and international agencies are at work for the reunion of Christendom.

This is not very startling but it did mean that in some areas local groups were beginning to form, and in 1938 the Friends of Reunion called for a national campaign to prepare people for unity. They saw their main target as the establishment of a network of ministers' fraternals around the country and also the formation of councils of Christian congregations. They also wanted to attract more young people to the cause. Here they were helped by their close connection with the Student Christian Movement which gave them good contacts. They were also pursuing a policy of speaking in theological colleges of all denominations, and raising union matters at diocesan conferences and similar places. The bulletin began to contain more material about local unity initiatives. Then the war interrupted the momentum which was clearly developing at this time.

But the Friends of Reunion were not alone. The 1930s was also the period during which plans were being made for the establishment of the British Council of Churches and the World Council of Churches. Who were making these plans? One of the key people in this country was, of course, William Temple, others were William Paton and J. H. Oldham, but many were the same people who made up the executive committee of the Friends of Reunion. They were acting officially through their churches to support unity as well as unofficially through the Friends of Reunion. By 1940 the group's membership was nearly 900; it never went very much higher than this, but its influence was much wider than its membership would suggest. And it was at the instigation of the Friends of Reunion that the SCM Press in 1941 published *Christian Reunion* by Hugh Martin, a book which can still be regarded as a major piece of apologetic for the ecumenical movement.

In the post-war period the Friends of Reunion persevered in the group's aims, but in a sense it had been too successful. Much of what it had begun had now been taken over by the British Council of Churches. Uncertainty about the group's role became a continuing concern as its members tried to reshape and reorganize it. The magazine became more intellectual – almost one continuous book review. A drive for new members in the early 1960s was reasonably successful but now unity as such was considered to be 'a good thing'. Councils of Churches had sprouted up everywhere. The ecumenical movement had become respectable. The time had come for the Friends of Reunion to come to an end, and in an act which some of the founder members regarded as fully in accord with its original intentions, it did so. This part of the story must now be told, but before this some other facts will have to be examined.

The pattern of a pressure group on the ecclesiastical front has always existed in some form or another. The Evangelical Revival provides several examples of this. One of them led to the establishment of a new denomination, the Methodist Church, and this is always one of the risks of such an activity. The Church of England has for long been pressurized by both an evangelical and an Anglo-Catholic party, each of which has tried to move the Church of England in its own direction. On the whole this activity, especially by the Anglo-Catholics, has been a very political one, and it is doubtful how valuable this has been. Professor Donald MacKinnon is surely right when he condemns the Anglo-Catholic agitation over the Church of South India as an extremely scandalous action, and he puts his finger on the reason for this when he writes:

> Issues of truth are obscured by the weapons men and women use to fight them. Of the spirit manifested in this episode one's verdict must be that it bore no mark at all of that manner of concern for ultimate truth on which, in the Christian's understanding of the Church's Lord, the Father has set his seal: I mean that witness to the truth which no more relies on the compulsive power of superior propaganda than it does on that of physical force, but which leaves the issue open, and is receptive, expectant, always seeking to fulfil the law of self-emptying.[1]

It has been the failure of these parties to act in an open way that justifies John Baker's comment that the Church of England does not demonstrate comprehensiveness but polarization, which is both stultifying and negative.[2]

There have emerged since the last war various other pressure groups in the churches which, just because they have been committed to renewal and ecumenism, have not succumbed to the dangers which Professor MacKinnon has exposed. The earliest of these was the Congregational Church Order Group formed in the 1940s which worked for liturgical revision in Congregationalism, and for a higher doctrine of the church, which the group saw to be part of the denomination's origin. It has pressed for church unity and for closer involvement with the world. It contained some of the ablest and most articulate of the Congregational ministers. In a sense they became the establishment, and in more recent years the group came to see that renewal was an ecumenical and not a denominational function.

The Presbyterians in England have never organized themselves so fully, but some of them participated in the Congregational Church Order Group and others are members of the Iona Community. The role of the Iona Community, under the leadership of George MacLeod, as a force for renewal in Scotland has been well documented and is well known. It has now entered a new and more difficult phase, but it has so far avoided becoming part of the establishment in the Church of Scotland.

Parish and People was an Anglican organization which came into existence in 1949 under the guidance of Gabriel Hebert of the Society of the Sacred Mission, Kelham, to promote and apply to the Church of England. the principles of the liturgical movement on the continent. It established a local network in Anglican dioceses, but the main work was done through its journal and through conferences on liturgical themes. Here again the initial aim was achieved; the new liturgical pattern swept through the Church of England. In 1963 Parish and People merged with the Keble Conference Group to work for the reform of the Church of England, not least in renewal of the parish ministry. It also took over the work of the Advisory Group on Christian Cells. It then appointed a full-time director, Eric James, and under his leadership the movement became much more broadly-based, but still committed to mission and renewal. The highlight of this period was its promotion in Britain of of the World Council of Churches study on the missionary structure of the congregation which we shall examine later. Thus the movement also gained an ecumenical base.

The Methodist Renewal Group began in 1961 when two ministers, Robin Sharp and John Vincent, got together with some of their friends to see how Methodism might be opened up to new ideas and to the world in general. They committed themselves to theological study, a common discipline of prayer, experimental worship and to discovering ways of Christian political action and new means of evangelism. They also had a regional organization and held an annual conference which was the focal point of their activities. Their magazine *New Directions* was a very sharp piece of journalism which attacked many of the sacred cows within Methodism and outside it. The renewal group also discovered how to manipulate the monolithic procedures of the Methodist Conference, and the Methodist establishment was forced to take notice of it and subsequently in a rather patronizing way to make use of it. Of all the renewal groups, this one had the strongest social and political sense. It, too, began to see that it could not remain solely as a denominational agency and it proposed a merger with Parish and People after they had run a joint conference together in 1968.

A group of Baptist ministers in the Midlands met to discuss what they considered to be the very poor Baptist response to the Nottingham Faith and Order Conference of 1964. The result of this was a book entitled *Baptists for Unity*, which called for a much deeper ecumenical commitment from Baptists. The Baptist Renewal Group emerged out of a conference which met in December 1968 to discuss this report. This group has worked for a more open and radical approach to the renewal of the Baptist denomination. It has a regional organization and holds an annual conference as well as producing papers on various aspects of the work of the Baptist Church.

Apart from the Friends of Reunion, most of these groups have been predominantly clerical in their membership and motivation. This is not true of the Catholic Renewal Movement, which has been much more of a lay movement and is probably the largest of the groups with which we are concerned here. Following the second Vatican Council, many Catholic lay people looked forward to considerable radical change in the Roman Catholic Church. As time went on, while many changes were made, they became disillusioned and frustrated by what was happening in this highly authoritarian church. This frustration reached its peak with the publication of the Papal Encyclical *Humanae Vitae* in August 1968. Many groups of Catholics protested against the Pope's failure to take the advice of his own experts or really to understand how most people felt about marriage. In January 1969 a national conference, drawn from a large number of these groups, resulted in the formation of the Catholic Renewal Movement. It saw that the birth control issue was simply a symptom of a much deeper problem of the nature and exercise of authority in the Roman Catholic Church. It took a strong stand on behalf of the priests who were suspended as a result of their protest against the encyclical, and has seen most of the protesters reinstated. The emphasis of the Catholic Renewal Movement has been on the establishment of local groups, and its attention is concentrated on local problems in the church. It publishes a regular bulletin, and has also issued further statements and reports; the most significant to date have been a statement in favour of family planning and a detailed examination and critique of Catholic schools. It is also committed to working

32

ecumenically, but is very much aware of the massive task which it faces in its own church.

So it can be seen that quite a considerable effort in all the denominations has been put into the work of renewal and reform. The way in which this has worked out has varied greatly. Many within them will not be aware of how much the movements have achieved just by their existence. Nevertheless, to change massive ecclesiastical structures takes a great deal of effort, any institution is very well equipped to suffocate or neutralize those working for radical change. The most serious example of this has been the institutionalizing of ecumenism within the structures of the British Council of Churches and local councils of churches so that it has all become dull and impotent; but we shall examine this later.

In 1967 John Weller, Faith and Order Secretary of the British Council of Churches, saw the need for the renewal groups to meet together, and he invited the Friends of Reunion to take action to convene such meetings. These took place regularly, and after two or three the need to establish a new pattern of renewal became evident. Many of the groups were suffering as a result of their own success. 'Much of what we campaigned for,' wrote John Hammersley, Executive Secretary of Parish and People, 'has been taken into the system, and we have had our teeth drawn.'[3] There was a need for something new and broader. As all the renewal movements were committed to unity it seemed natural that they should unite. The Methodist Renewal Group and Parish and People thought it important to unite as a witness to the proposed Anglican-Methodist Unity. The Friends of Reunion conducted a survey of its members and discovered that a very large number of them were over seventy years of age. They were people who in early days had seen an ecumenical vision and had remained faithful to it, but they were not now in a position to take much action. The survey also asked what the future of the Friends of Reunion should be, and as a result of the replies the secretary was able to comment as follows:

> The justification for an 'unofficial' body can only be that it is there to do 'unofficial' things; and on the ecumenical front, as well as the mission front, there are plenty of unofficial things to be done. The gospel is demanding that pioneers and experimenters should do what the established churches will not do in attempting new forms of mission, creating new ecumenical patterns which question accepted positions and help to analyse the large amount of lay frustration which has been revealed in all the churches by such exercises as 'The People Next Door'. Moreover the manpower which is available throughout the country through the membership of the renewal groups together is very considerable. It should be possible to find a new pattern of likeminded people in many localities to act as 'ginger groups' or task forces to act ecumenically to further mission and unity outside and within the existing structure.

He thought this would provide a means of mutual support for people and a base for local activity. The Friends of Reunion accepted this proposal and put it, in a slightly more refined form, to a meeting of all the renewal groups. As a result of this a working party was set up to take these suggestions further. The result of this was that in June 1969 Parish and People, the Methodist and Baptist Renewal Groups, the Congregational Church Order Group and the Friends of Reunion announced that they intended to cease to be independent organizations and to support the new movement which would be launched in January 1970. The Roman Catholic Newman Association, the Catholic Renewal Movement and the William Temple Association also participated in the venture. The working party proposed the establishment of a 'Proto-Council' consisting of representatives of the participating bodies who would work out the details of the movement and launch it in its final form.

This was an act of faith. It was not clear what the Proto-Council would be able to do or who would be interested in it. The more cynical members thought that even if they did not launch anything they had at least killed off some fairly redundant organizations. The Proto-Council turned out to be an interesting body containing some of the more elderly renewers who had been around for a long time and some younger more revolutionary people. Hence the Proto-Council entered into a debate about revolution or reformation as the style of the movement. It decided that this was not a problem to be resolved but that essentially the movement was concerned with helping people to 'do their own thing' and to be accepted by others in doing it.

A great deal of time was spent on constitutional matters and in drawing up a statement of intent for the movement. Nor was it clear what the movement should be called. Finally in November after a great deal of work the Proto-Council decided that they could do no more. The details had been sorted out, the declaration prepared, a conference arranged and the financial matters satisfactorily settled. They were either to go ahead not knowing what would happen or to stop at this point. They decided that there was nothing to lose but everything to gain by going ahead. The movement was to be called 'ONE for Christian Renewal'. The declaration of the movement read:

As members of a world in revolution,
a divided church,
a generation for which forgiveness and love alone have authority,
WE COMMIT OURSELVES
– to accept one another in Christ
– to study together the nature of our responsibility for God's world
– to combat poverty, racialism and oppression through social and political action
– to help in re-creating the one church new in witness, worship and life
– to support actively those doing the work of Christ inside or outside the institutional church
– to ground our action for renewal in our own situation
– to underwrite this commitment financially.

Newsletters were sent to all members of the existing groups

and they were invited to come to the inaugural Spring Bank Holiday conference. Many enrolled, others waited to see what would happen at the conference.

The conference proved to be an unusual event attended by over 300 people. The highlight of it was a conference eucharist where there was no celebrant and everyone communicated including the Roman Catholics who were there. The liturgy had been very carefully prepared and was for many an expression of what ONE is all about: namely a determination to accept one another in Christ and be free to express the Christian faith in many diverse ways. Also at Swanwick a Council was elected and a tentative network of regional groups was set up. ONE is not asking people to do new things but to be free to do what they see to be right with any who will act with them. The main function of ONE is to be a supportive network for many who are committed to the Christian faith but not committed to its present institutional expressions. Through a newsletter the Council is trying to provide ONE members with information about each other and ideas of things to do. It also tries through D (denominational) groups to influence the decision-making bodies of the churches. To date the most effective of these have been the Baptist and Methodist groups.

Some local groups are meeting for the sharing of ideas and mutual support, others are arranging conferences and big public meetings on specific issues. Others are just doing what they did before with the realization that they are not alone but have a network of support behind them. To assist in this the Council is producing a directory of all members so that they may be encouraged to meet each other and get in touch with people who have like interests to their own.

The Council is also concerned about theological issues and is trying to provide kits which will enable people to 'do theology' in a new way.

36

The story of ONE is not a great success story. It is still not clear what the way ahead is going to be. Its membership is not large, the level of commitment varies greatly and so far no issues have emerged on which it can campaign on a wide front. All this may be no bad thing; the story has been told here to show how on an ecumenical basis one group of people is trying to find what might be called 'an alternative church' – a new pattern of Christian living which allows flexibility and freedom within a context of common acceptance and wide social concern. It is not an attempt to overthrow the existing church, but an attempt by seeking an alternative to set free some dynamic of change which will enable the church to find new life and expression for itself. John Pairman Brown in his book *The Liberated Zone*,[4] which in many ways goes beyond this and seems to be moving towards extracting Christians out of present-day society, sums up this attitude to the institution which ONE would also accept when he argues that there is no need to leave the institutional church unless you are pushed out. The main thing is to act in freedom and sit lightly to the church.[5]

There are many other groups of likeminded people in the churches, the most highly organized of which must be the Evangelical Alliance which is one of the oldest interdenominational organizations in Britain. This exists to promote and defend evangelical Christianity. Some members of ONE also belong to the Evangelical Alliance and the Alliance's recent report *On the Other Side*, the investigation of missionary activity, and their analysis of the New Town situation, are very open and forward looking.

The tradition of the religious community, both monastic and more informal like the Lee Abbey community, also expresses attempts to establish different patterns of Christian life and mission. History shows us that these movements either become institutionalized and therefore part of the new definition of the Church or they become centres of schism. Early Methodism, which was an attempt to renew the Church of England, led to many divisions. The Salvation Army itself became an independent body because of its rejection by Methodism, whereas the Society of Jesus, which might well have gone the same way, is still a power within the Roman Catholic Church. Those who fear that new movements may create new denominations are in fact the people who may cause this to happen. But where there can be real acceptance of each other and a real understanding of the need for new patterns for church life, the tension between renewal movements and the institutional church can be creative. This can only be the case, however, when there is willingness on both sides to accept new insights and to be open to new truths. Once people make an exclusive claim to possess the truth or to be right, schism becomes inevitable. Christian division is caused not by heresy but by the attitude of mind that is closed to new ideas and new truths. The creative attitude does not take the church too seriously but is prepared to follow Christ in openness and expectancy.

II

The question of attitudes of mind leads on to the question which many people are asking today and which was the subject of one of the Sections of the Uppsala Assembly of the World Council of Churches, *Towards a New Style of Living*. For many the old patterns of Christian prayer and worship have little meaning in today's world. Ecumenism has a part to play here. There are some signs that attempts to find new life and to renew man's spirit are beginning to bear fruit.

At an earlier stage the churches together were able to enter upon an approach which might be called 'comparative spirituality' whereby Christians were greatly enriched by sharing in and using the devotional methods of each other's traditions. Under the influence of such people as Evelyn Underhill and Baron Von Hugel the attractions of a 'Catholic' spirituality spread far and wide. Its influence can be seen in the Iona Community, in the Methodist Sacramental Fellowship and in other reformed traditions. There can be little doubt that many gained much from this but today this does not seem to be enough. Olive Wyon in her book *Living Springs*[6] gave a useful survey of developing patterns of Christian community life which had at its centre the need for new patterns of Christian living and prayer. Many of the communities she described are still thriving and have a strong ecumenical base, not least the Taizé Community, whose contribution to ecumenism is now widely known. Others like the Grail and Lee Abbey have a growing ecumenical commitment as part of their life.

For the average churchgoer the one time when he is faced with questions of this sort is in the Week of Prayer for Christian Unity. The observance of this week is fairly universal in Britain but is at present going through a difficult phase. After gradually building up during the 1960s the week has reached a point when people are not sure what to do with it. At one time it was used as an occasion for people to hold public meetings to talk about unity. These meetings have now been replaced by much smaller groups, often meeting in houses, to discuss ecumenical concerns like those reported from Godalming in chapter 1. In other places the emphasis of the week has moved from the word 'unity' to the word 'prayer'. What does it mean to pray today? Is there a God to pray to anyhow? How does prayer relate to everyday life? These are the questions which Christians wish to ask and need help in considering. The questions are common to all Christians regardless of denomination and they provide a basis for dealing with fundamental issues of the Christian faith.

Concern and interest in prayer is not limited to those in the churches. One of the interesting phenomena of the present 'pop scene' is its interest in meditation, the occult, new experience and questions of personal identity. Moreover there is also a growing interest in new patterns of community living which can help people to break through the impersonal nature of so much of modern life. Not all communities have a right basis, they can be the means whereby people preserve themselves from involvement in reality. Community life can be very creative for people for periods in their growth even if not permanently. Some communities like Pilsdon and the Cyreneans have been set up deliberately to provide a basis of therapeutic living for people who have personality problems.

We have already made reference to the Farncombe Community at Godalming. This is an ecumenical order for women which owed its origin to a group who had worked together in the Church of South India. It was established at Farncombe in 1963 and has grown slowly but steadily, and there are now seven members including one Roman Catholic. They lead a life of prayer and study together with some involvement in the local community. They also address meetings on ecumenical affairs, take quiet days and retreats. In Godalming and the surrounding area they provide a firm foundation for ecumenical growth in a very quiet and unassuming way.

There is a need today for centres where people can come together to learn to pray, to express their common concerns and to experiment in new patterns of worship and prayer. It was this conviction together with a concern to improve the quality of Free Church spirituality which led Norman James to establish an Ecumenical House for Prayer at Benifold near Haslemere. This was an act of faith which took place after very careful consultation and discussion. The aim of the house was to be a place where groups from churches or mixed groups might come for ecumenical retreat or for an experimental weekend of their own devising. Norman James and his wife gathered round them a small staff to help run the house which thus provided a basic pattern of daily prayer at the house, and through a group of associates maintained a pattern of prayer for the house. There is no common rule of life, but a pattern of mutual concern and intercession for one another. The Warden also made himself available to talk about spirituality around the country and also to conduct retreats. The house provoked considerable interest and was used by many groups – but more by Anglicans than by others. Many people liked to use the house for their own programmes; those who wished to attend the events provided by the staff were fewer in number. Individual guests also came from time to time. As time went on it became clear that the house was not fully viable financially and after discussion the house was finally sold. But that is not the end of the story. The Benifold experience has provided a lot of information about the spiritual needs of people and the role of a house of prayer in relation to them. Moreover, the Benifold organization is still in existence. Norman James is still the Warden and now with a travelling brief is looking at the role of many centres and the forms in which contemporary spirituality is emerging. It may be that at some future date there will be another centre established on the basis of the Benifold experience. It is equally possible that existing conference centres and retreat houses may be used to promote an ecumenical understanding about prayer and about God. John Baker has reminded us that there is a vital need for this which must underpin schemes for organic union of the churches:

> Small cells of the *un*likeminded, however unimportant they are by worldly standards, who want to explore into God together and come

41

to a new and shared understanding, must have the arrogance to decide to do so, whether others will hear or whether they will forbear.[7]

The development of such groups can take place anywhere. Sometimes such groups come to a new discovery of the reality of prayer not through particular disciplines but within a group which is deeply concerned for others. To agonize over the needs of others, for instance in a local Amnesty group, is itself an act of intercession because the goal is victory or release for the other. In such groups as these which may not be formally Christian in membership, people who say that they find God to be unreal become conscious of working with God.

At the same time a considerable number of young people are entirely 'traditional' in their pattern of spirituality and they must not be dismissed as unrealistic. One of the groups of 'unlikeminded' who need to be kept together are the 'traditionalist' and the 'radical'. This is just as important as bringing together the members of different denominations. In the student world, when church allegiance is maintained, there is more denominationalism than ecumenism, but this is not necessarily detrimental either to deep Christian commitment or to an openness which begins within the institution of the church instead of outside it.

There are reports of several new Christian communities emerging at the moment. Some are simply the result of enthusiasm of a few and will not last long. Others are more formally established with denominational backing or support. The influence of Nicholas Ferrar and his seventeenth-century community at Little Gidding still survives in the Pilsdon community and in the Little Gidding Fellowship, some of whose members are considering the establishment of a new ecumenical community there. There are Christian hippy communes emerging; there are other less formal

42

groupings of those with common concerns who meet occasionally.

At Haywards Heath in Sussex one of the Cowley Fathers, Herbert Slade, is running a house whose main concern is to relate the techniques of eastern meditation to the Christian faith. Those who go there to learn are finding new insights and new strength through his work.

In Edinburgh the Fraternity of the Transfiguration, an Anglican group with a very simple pattern of life and strong emphasis on prayer and meditation, has found itself invaded by many young people who

'have been to the east' – either literally or culturally they have an amalgam of Hindu, Buddhist and Islamic mystical tradition. They all travel with I-Ching and have all the profoundest respect and some thirst for the Christian mystical tradition when it is discovered. They are non-society, non-established, non-church, etc. Many are un-reconciled with bewildered, worldly parents.[8]

Some of them are now living a community life alongside the Fraternity.

It may be that the ecumenical movement has got to take prayer a lot more seriously. The Abbé Couturier's vision, great as it was, now needs to go further, so that as Christians together 'explore into God' they thus find unity not only with each other, but unity with many in the world who in their search for identity and meaning turn to prayer and meditation to find it.

III

Olive Wyon noted that the communities she examined had various things in common. They were concerned for the renewal of their own denomination, concerned for effective mission, and for Christian unity. They were committed to prayer, solitude and silence and to a single-mindedness given in holiness to God. In this chapter we have looked at some of the renewal groups and some of the new attempts at community and patterns of spirituality without which ecumenism would be dead. Behind it all we see the development not of a single pattern but of a new attitude of mind which takes the world seriously and sits lightly to the institutional church. David Jenkins has called for a Christian *ascesis* which will help us to cope with the *askewness* of the church. This askewness shows itself in Christian division, in the dominance of the institution over people, in a lack of openness and a refusal to face reality. We hope we have shown that there are signs that this ascesis may be beginning to appear in those who find in Christ a freedom which enables them to accept those who hold opposing views and who see the need to create an alternative church in order to change the institution; who are concerned for social justice but above all who are always willing to be open to the truth instead of thinking that they already possess it. Without this attitude there can be no unity locally or nationally. This is why Christian spirituality is an essential part of Christian unity.

NOTES

1. D. McKinnon, *The Stripping of the Altars*, Collins 1968, pp.21–2. See also the article by F. Absalom on 'The Anglo-Catholic Priest: Aspects of Role Conflict' in M. Hill (ed.), *A Sociological Yearbook of Religion in Britain 4*, SCM Press 1971.

2. J. A. Baker, *The Foolishness of God*, Darton, Longman and Todd 1970, p.372.

3. J. Hammersley, 'The New Movement' in *New Directions*, New Series Vol. I No. 4, 1969, p.4.

4. John Pairman Brown, *The Liberated Zone*, SCM Press 1970.

5. For details about 'ONE for Christian Renewal' contact B. Brailey, 'Lomehurst', 191 Creighton Avenue, London N2 9SZ.

6. O. Wyon, *Living Springs*, SCM Press 1963.

7. *The Foolishness of God*, p.372.

8. R. Walls, 'The Fraternity of the Transfiguration', *New Fire* No. 6, Spring 1971, p.24.

3 PND and All That

I

The Nottingham Faith and Order Conference of 1964 marks a watershed in British ecumenical history. It had been prepared for over a long period in various ways including local study programmes and regional conferences. People at all levels of church life were involved and the conference assembled with great expectancy. The dramatic resolution of the conference was that calling on the churches to covenant together to achieve organic unity by 1980. This resolution has been much criticized, but the reason why nothing came of it in England was really because no one did sufficient work to follow it up. The resolution as such was not at fault, and this is clearly shown by the effective way in which the churches in Wales are moving towards such a covenant with conviction and a reasonable hope of success.

Another resolution was about the designation of areas of ecumenical experiment and we shall look at this in chapter 5. There were other significant aspects of the conference, not least the debate about intercommunion, but David Edwards[1] pointed out that the main pointers for the future lay in the discussion about the proper shape for the church for the future if it is really to share in God's mission to the world. This is expressed in the resolution proposed by David Paton calling for an examination of the missionary situation in Britain. The ecumenical movement has always had as its basis the concern for mission and the Nottingham Conference reaffirmed this, not in terms of mission overseas but of mission in Britain.

This concern reflected a study of the World Council of Churches which had been initiated at New Delhi in 1961 on the missionary structure of the congregation. By the time the Nottingham Conference took place news about the way this study was going was beginning to emerge and great interest was being shown in it. Odd copies of a book published in America, *Where in the World?*, by Colin Williams,[2] were being circulated. John Robinson in his book *The New Reformation*[3] made some reference to the study.

These two events, the Nottingham Conference and the WCC study, came together in the People Next Door programme which took place in 1967. The story of this programme has already been well described in the report *Agenda for the Churches*.[4] It is important to understand the origins of the programme.

In 1965 the Church of England conducted a major study programme on mission entitled 'No Small Change'. Nearly 7,000 parishes took part and the material was designed for use in groups over a period of six weeks. It led to a growing missionary awareness, though it must be said that this has been expressed more in activity at home than in greatly increased support for the church overseas. It also produced considerable lay frustration when the church seemed impotent to implement the recommendations which came from the study groups. But the study itself was a success and others wished to use a similar technique for ecumenical study.

At the same time the British Council of Churches was trying to work out how to follow up the Nottingham Conference. Moreover, the Conference of British Missionary Societies wanted to promote some study on mission in an ecumenical setting. There were reports of other groups, like Parish and People, also considering launching a study programme. An awareness developed in church headquarters that there was a danger of local congregations being swamped with study material. As a result a decision was taken to launch one common programme to be used ecumenically in the spring of 1967; this became 'The People Next Door'.

A long period of planning and preparation began in the summer of 1965 and the first main decision was that the course should be on the lines of the World Council of Churches Study on the missionary structure of the congregation, which in 1966 has produced a report entitled *The Church for Others*.[5] An editorial group produced the material, which included a background book for group leaders, filmstrips, role plays and survey material. The programme was deliberately designed to help the church people to see what was going on in the world around them and what questions the world was putting to the churches.

A training programme was also launched whereby three-day meetings were held in over a dozen centres where people went through the material and were given some understanding of working with small groups. Those who attended these meetings became the nucleus for local training throughout the country. This training took place in the autumn of 1966; most of the study groups began in February 1967.

In the end, either that spring or later, between 80,000 and 100,000 people took part in the programme. This number was much smaller than had been expected, but where the programme was seriously taken up its impact was very considerable.

The effects of the PND programme have been very wide and have contributed to the growing use of house groups by the churches. One immediate result was the rapid growth in the number of local councils of churches. Between 1967 and

1969 they increased from 500 to nearly 700. This is an average of about two a week for two years, whereas in the previous two years the rate had been exactly half this. Thus a wider ecumenical network was established.

One of the chief requests coming from the programme was the demand for intercommunion and there has been a considerable growth in intercommunion services between Anglicans and others in the succeeding years. The programme also marked the arrival of Roman Catholics on the local ecumenical scene in a new way. From then on they have been increasingly involved and now play an active part in 73 per cent of local councils of churches.

The programme also led to considerable social action by councils of churches, mainly in terms of 'Good Neighbour' schemes, road wardens and the visiting of the old and the sick. In other areas joint magazines and newspapers by the churches have been established.

One issue which emerged must be regarded as a major problem and that is clergy–laity relations. One group put it like this:

> In many churches a structure has developed which depends entirely on the minister. His central position has determined the activities of the congregation. His concerns and interests become also those of his congregation. This limits the activities, and many laymen feel that there is no scope there to contribute their interests and abilities to the life of the church. In the local community, it is the layman, not the minister, who has the wider experience and the greater authority. In the life of the local church the layman has a positive, radical, and indeed revolutionary part to play. He must find what is his own particular task and the church must nourish and train him for his work and uphold him in it.[6]

We shall see later that this is one of the most intractable problems in church life today.

The other approach to mission which was opened up by the People Next Door programme and also by *The Church for Others* has been by means of surveys. Part of the programme was to engage in some very minor survey of the resources of the church in their own area, and this led some to decide to conduct more thorough surveys of their area. One of the most interesting was that of eight churches in North Oxford conducted by the council of churches there. This was a survey of the churches' resources. It revealed that the total church-going population could easily be housed in two of the churches and that the plant was not being adequately used. Perhaps one day the churches will have the courage to implement some of the obvious conclusions from this survey. This approach is now being used in other places but what is required is a commitment to implement the findings of the survey.

II

1966 also saw the conference at Saltley jointly sponsored by the British Council of Churches and Parish and People to familiarize the churches in Britain with the findings in *The Church for Others*.[7] For many people, mainly clergy, this was a turning point in their lives. A survey of those who attended the conference which was conducted in 1969 revealed how significant this had been. Their replies also help us to give some brief glimpse of the findings contained in *The Church for Others*. They were asked three questions:

1. Has the study affected your theological thinking – if so in what way?
2. Has it affected the way you work?
3. Are you aware of experiments in mission which are based at least in part on the findings of the study?

Over a third of those who attended the conference replied and, while a few thought it had been a waste of time, the majority affirmed the value of the conference and the thinking behind it.

The longest answers came in reply to the first question.

A fairly typical answer (from an Anglican vicar) is the following:

> The idea of mission as God's mission, as something at work in the world to which the church is to witness, came over in a very liberating way. It clarified and opened up a subject about which I had felt unhappy (i.e. in its traditional formulations) and confused. The perspective offered by the word *shalom* I found helpful. Also the whole way in which the church was portrayed as the servant of the world: the order GOD – WORLD – CHURCH was really a final nail in the coffin of the triumphalist church.

A Methodist minister writes similarly:

> I think the chief theological benefit has been to provide a number of concepts that have helped to draw together a whole range of thinking, e.g. *shalom* has enabled me to build up a much larger conception of mission, proclamation and service etc.; *missio dei*, emphasising the ongoing activity of God which I have been able to link with renewed theological interest in 'hope'; *morphological fundamentalism*, clarifying the theological basis of change. It seems to me that jargon words and phrases, so often derided, are not to be used too much except as points around which to cluster and bring to unity a number of ideas.

The concept of the human zone as the area in which most people live most of their lives and therefore the basic unit for missionary strategy also caused considerable interest.

The second question produced signs of activity in new directions. One Anglican archdeacon went straight back and included some of the material in his charges to church-wardens in his area. There are several references to decisions not to build new church buildings; one Anglican vicar wrote:

> By the end of the century ... X ... is planned to expand to 110,000 – the Saltley Conference contributed to my decision not to erect an Anglican building in the immediate future in one of the expanding villages in my parish. We are going to use the community centre which the village has just built for itself.

Several others reported that the conference had contributed to their decision to centre their work in the area of community relations and community development. One Roman Catholic priest gave up school teaching to do adult education work. Others thought it had affected their whole concept of ministry. A Methodist minister wrote:

> I find that I interpret ministry now in terms of facilitating and enabling; providing the possibilities of reconciliation and development in individuals and society. The traditional statements and controversies about ministry seem more and more remote and irrelevant . . . The study . . . has moved me on to take community development techniques seriously, and to develop a non-directive approach. I find all this puts me between the congregation and the community, and a process of interpretation between the two. I can no longer see myself as related only to the congregation, and in that relation predominantly authoritative and supporting. I have become, at least in a faltering way, interpreter, facilitator, enabler, resource provider, in a fairly wide sector of the local community.

This comment illustrates a new attitude to ministry which would enable people to discover that style of life which will set them free today.

The replies to the third question were less forthcoming. This may well reflect the slowness at which it is possible to implement change. One writer comments:

> In this diocese . . . there was produced a serious report on the challenges and problems of the seventies. It was in many ways influenced by the kind of thinking Saltley encouraged. End product: nil, because again it would have meant heart-searching and the dismantling of a good deal of established organization.

Thus while the impact of the study on people's thinking has been considerable, it has not yet had its full effect on action. We hope that the rest of this book will show how it is beginning to impinge upon the way people are acting. But no one factor is ever dominant; one of the main pressures on the church is that of population growth and economic necessity, and this is as important in bringing out new approaches to mission and theological reflection.

There is little doubt that the missionary structure thinking came to Britain at the right moment but that it now needs to be taken further. Thus one correspondent who was at Saltley has pungently summed up the situation in these words:

> The missionary structure study was really about assumptions. I feel that some of these assumptions are now much more widely accepted than a few years ago. This may be less to do with direct influence of the WCC, Williams, Hoekendijk, Margull, etc., etc., than with the fact that people were beginning to come up with similar ideas at about the same time. But what worries me is that there is little theological depth about the mission discussion at the moment. We have taken the point about starting with concrete situations and letting theology develop, but we seem to be scared (in Britain anyway) of having a good full-blooded theological ding-dong.

Ecumenism does *not* mean funking areas of disagreement. So we come back again to the need for the right attitudes and assumptions for unity and for mission. We also see articulated here the need for Christians to express open and honest disagreement with each other. Partly because of the polarization which has taken place in Britain between the 'ecumenical' attitude on the one hand and the 'evangelical' on the other, this facing of disagreement has not really come into the open yet. When it does we shall almost certainly see that there are many other attitudes to be discovered here, not least among those who find their security and identity in the *status quo* and who would not like to be called either evangelical or ecumenical.

III

Both *The Church for Others* and PND had plenty of critics. PND was seen by some as a form of humanism. The clergy did not like it because they were excluded from the groups and so could not tell people what the answers were. One of the main discoveries of PND was the fact that 'church people' as church people found it very difficult to keep in contact with non-churchgoers or to talk over the issues of PND (which were by no means merely ecclesiastical) with them. Many reported that this aspect of the course was impossible. This finding only confirmed the premise of *The Church for Others* that the church congregations, far from being mission-centred, were extremely introverted and concerned for their own life rather than the life of the world.

But it is here that the debate about mission begins. Is the church concerned to build up its own life or is it to build up the life of the world? Many would reply that this is not an 'either/or' but a 'both/and'. Nevertheless the starting point is very important. If we are concerned about the life of the congregation all the time we are unlikely to do much for the community. If our concern is for the community, then it may be the life of the congregation will suffer. It may be, however, that there is a third way: if the congregation has a freedom and a 'secret discipline'[8] which sends it out into the community, then both may be considerably enriched.

The strongest criticisms of *The Church for Others* in Britain have come from Phillip Crowe and Douglas Webster. Crowe makes three main criticisms of the report.[9]

First of all, he thinks that there is in it a basic misunderstanding of the gospel. The work of Christ is regarded as a past event and not as a present reality. This comes, he says, from the refusal of the report to regard the Bible as an authoritative and permanent guide. Hence the gospel is seen as the departure point for mission rather than as its determinative content. The saving events of Christ, he says, are of eternal significance and must apply as much today as in the past. To say that Christ's work is completed and that all men are in the 'New Mankind' is just not true.

This objection is not new, but it does highlight one of the major debates of our time. How is scripture to be used? How determinative is it for us today? It is to be hoped that those scholars who are asking these questions at the moment will soon begin to examine the ecclesiological and missiological significance of what they are saying. Crowe's view, which would be accepted by many, seems to imply that Christianity is not really subject to the conditions of history, society or culture. Nor in his terms would it appear that Christianity has had any effect upon history and this would seem to deny the dynamic effects of the gospel which he is so anxious to preserve. The gospel, if it has changed the lives of people, must, in fact, change in expression itself. As Johannes Weiss put it:

> Most of us, in fact, have not passed over from Judaism or heathen-ism to Christianity; we have not first learned the gospel upon the heights of conscious life, after having lived in a period of darkness.[10]

The expressions of the gospel are bound to change as society changes. The missionary structure study is trying to say this and is trying to help the church to escape from forms and patterns of life which relate to a past age and not to today.

Phillip Crowe's second objection is that he thinks the study gravely exaggerates the way in which individuals are moulded by society. He admits that in the past evangelicals have not given sufficient weight to the influence of society on people, but he thinks the study goes too far the other way. The WCC study involved encounter between sociologists and theologians, and from this came a new understanding of the great extent to which social pressures mould people's lives. Is not the reverse a more serious danger? If all the church's effort is concentrated on individuals is there not a risk of extracting them out of society instead of committing them to it? The effects of excessive individualism in society can be very damaging. Moreover we are members one of another and concern for the well-being of our brother may well involve political action to improve the life of society throughout the world. We cannot limit our concerns purely to those of the individual.

Thirdly, Phillip Crowe thinks that the study fails to safeguard the essentials of the missionary task. Evangelism is not seen as central, the saving events of Christ must be proclaimed if men are to be saved. It cannot be argued that service is proclamation because God's action for man's redemption must be announced, and this is not just done by service. The heart of mission, he argues, lies in the proclaiming what God has done and calling men to repentance. Thus while mission and service must go together, proclamation is their basic justification.

Such a sharp distinction between proclamation and service really seems to lead to a debasement of proclamation. There is little virtue in the type of mass evangelism which takes place at little cost to the proclaimer and without sufficient context to be really creative. The gospel requires a context in which it can be spoken; this is more likely to come out of dialogue and action and will determine the way in which the gospel is proclaimed. To make a sharp distinction between evangelism and service militates against this. Many would agree with R. G. Jones and A. Wesson when they argue:

> The actual methods employed by the church to proclaim her message will vary with the situation, but as far as possible she will seek to do it by means of dialogue. Monologue preaching may still have a place within the Christian community, but as an instrument of mission it is finished.[11]

Moreover, unless proclamation is authenticated in action and life it is an empty thing and this sharp distinction does not assist an understanding of this.

Douglas Webster, who has done so much to promote concern and interest in mission, has attacked the idea of the *missio dei*.[12] We cannot see all events in history as the action of God. He quotes the obvious examples of civil wars,

Belsen, Hiroshima and the like as acts which are clearly not the actions of God in history. He would like to see more emphasis on the role of evil in history. Nor, he says, is it right for us to say that everything which we approve of is part of the mission of God and those things which we disapprove of are not.

This is a major issue and the debate in the church today about how far the processes of secularization are part of God's activity is a very complex one. Certainly some theologians have been far too optimistic about secularization and so demonstrate a new sort of evolutionary determinism. This assumes that what has happened in the Western process of secularization is necessarily right and must be the same for all the world. But there is a distinction to be made between seeing God's action in history and seeing God's will always being done in history. An essential corollary to this sort of thinking is to realize the potentiality of every situation for good or for evil. The more man controls his environment the greater this potentiality becomes. The discovery of how to split the atom can lead to terrible evil (Hiroshima) or to terrific good (new sources of power). To share in the mission of God is not just to share in the events of the world but to work to release all the potentialities for good. A similar view was put forward in the seventeenth century, in relation to the devotional life, by a French Jesuit, Jean-Pierre de Caussade, who called on those who wish to seek holiness to abandon themselves to God in 'the sacrament of the present moment', and thus to bring good out of every event in life.

Douglas Webster goes on to criticize the report for its indifference to the matter of church growth. He thinks that it is only right that men and women who are brought to God 'will join the Christian community in corporate expressions of faith and worship'. He doubts whether Christian life can be sustained outside Christian fellowship and Christian sacrament and, while he realizes that the church is full of 'cultural baggage' which is no part of its essential nature,

It is impossible to have Christianity without the church or to retain the church without concern that it should grow.

But the report is concerned to show what the role of the church should be and it is not arguing that there is no need to convince people of the truth of the gospel. The anxiety is that the church has become so concerned with itself that it is denying the gospel it should proclaim. People's uncertainty about adding numbers to the church as it is springs from the fact that they cannot see the church obeying the gospel. One of the reasons for this is that the church claims too much for itself and not enough for God and his mission. Moreover, concern for identifiable numbers does not seem to be central to the Christian mission. No one is denying that the church will have to have some institutional expression; what is being doubted is whether the present institutional pattern can serve the mission of God. Thus John Taylor writes:

If we see the need to change from a parish-centred to a group-centred expression of our Christian discipleship, we must obey and go forward, not because it will make us more splendid Christians painlessly, but because the circumstances of these days suggest that is what our Lord is calling us to do, however difficult it may be.[13]

Webster also doubts whether many Christians will be in a position to influence the structures of their society. He quotes such places as Thailand, Russia and Saudi Arabia. Certainly the approach of the church is these and other places will be very different from Western society, but this is exactly what *The Church for Others* is calling for. Thus the East Asia Christian Conference report *Structures for a Missionary Congregation* rightly comments:

Only out of the struggles of a local church in a specific *place* to be the church *in that place* can structures relevant to that place and situation emerge. They may well be more varied than we have ever known, for we live in a more complex world than ever before.[14]

The Church for Others is not saying that we know what these structures are but that we should endeavour to discover them. Concern for numbers militates against this attempt. This is not because there is anything wrong or right about numbers but because our concern is with the gospel and finding a new shape for the church in the world today. Interest in numbers inevitably leads to maintaining the present pattern only, so the identifiable numbers can be (somewhat unreliably) counted. It is much more a matter of what people are doing about their faith than whether they go to church or not that matters. Concern for numbers must mean a concern for numbers at worship within the present pattern of church life.

Thus *The Church for Others* is encouraging theological debate. But how far is it being tried in practice? The real test is whether the proposals envisaged here do in fact enable the gospel to be communicated and Christian living to be more of a reality today. This will take some time to show itself, but one thing which must already be clear is that there will be no one pattern. Just as the PND programme tried to help people to face their own situation and act on the basis of it, so the churches in different places and at different levels will need to find many varied expressions.

What both these exercises reported in this chapter show is that the pre-requisite for mission and for mission in unity is a strong realism about the situation in which we are at the moment, wherever we are. This will determine our action and the shape of the church. It is not necessary to agree with all the theology and jargon of the missionary structure to see this. Indeed the significant Evangelical Alliance report *On the Other Side*[15] shows this clearly. For here a study on modern means of evangelism begins with a sociological analysis of Britain today. Nor is this surprising, because those who wrote it were able to refer to *The Church for Others*. Whatever our theological position we must be honest about our own situation before we can do something about it. Such honesty is not easy to achieve, for people do not like too much reality. PND helped a little; much more help is needed.

One sociological study of the church which followed *The Church for Others* was that conducted in industrial South West Wales by the Blaendulais Ecumenical Centre. The report it produced, entitled *The Church in a Mobile Society*, analyses the region in terms of population, industry, power and the role of the churches, and makes recommendations for a zonal strategy. Its conclusions on the churches are as follows:

> The church is not dead – to suggest that it is is not merely a blasphemy but an insult to the loyalty and devotion of thousands of Christians. The church is not dead but alive, and not so much kicking as fighting – fighting thousands of heroic rearguard actions in isolated outposts – *with relatively little effect*.[16]

If we are realistic we will discover the truth of this statement in many places. We must now see in what ways the vast resources the churches still have at their disposal may be more creatively used.

NOTES

1. D. L. Edwards and R. E. Davies, *Unity Begins at Home*, SCM Press 1964, pp.48ff.
2. C. Williams, *Where in the World?*, Epworth 1966.
3. J. A. T. Robinson, *The New Reformation*, SCM Press 1965.
4. C. K. Sansbury and others, *Agenda for the Churches*, SCM Press 1968.
5. *The Church for Others*, WCC 1966.
6. *Agenda for the Churches*, p.50.
7. T. Beeson (ed.), *The World is the Agenda*, Parish and People 1966.
8. This is the term which Dietrich Bonhoeffer used to describe the devotional life of the church.

9. *Mission in the Modern World*, Patmos Press 1968, pp.12–29.

10. J. Weiss, *The History of Primitive Christianity*, Macmillan 1937 (reprinted as *Earliest Christianity*, Harper Torchbooks, USA 1959), Vol. II, p.442.

11. R. G. Jones and A. J. Wesson, *Towards a Radical Church*, Epworth 1970, p.115.

12. D. Webster, *Not Ashamed*, Hodder and Stoughton 1970, pp.101ff.

13. J. V. Taylor, *Breaking Down the Parish*, CMS 1968, p.12.

14. *Structures for a Missionary Congregation*, East Asia Christian Council 1964, pp.99–100.

15. *On the Other Side*, Scripture Union 1968.

16. V. Jones (ed.), *The Church in a Mobile Society*, C. Davies 1969, pp.99–100.

60

4 Local Councils of Churches

I

How does local ecumenical co-operation develop and what
are the snags? Today many people are bored with local
councils of churches and are wondering what can be done
about them. The British Council of Churches has recently
commended a report on this subject for study by the churches
and councils of churches. This report does not present a very
glowing view of the present situation. Its conclusion may be
summed up in the thesis that the establishment of a local
council of churches is the most effective way to prevent
ecumenism.

Even if this is in part true, councils of churches have
helped to further ecumenical awareness in Britain. Before we
examine four councils, it may help to summarize the procedures through which ecumenical co-operation normally
grows. The first stage of ecumenical co-operation consists in
Christians of different denominations in a locality being nice
to each other and acknowledging each other's existence. It is
not too long ago that even this did not happen. Thus in a
locality relationships normally begin because a matter of
common concern brings the churches together. All too often,
alas, this is a matter of protest. The churches wish to protest
about Sunday opening of shops, a new betting shop or something similar. In more recent years it has been the need to
promote the work of Christian Aid which has brought the
churches together. This leads on to other activities, the most

obvious of which is the Week of Prayer for Christian Unity. This week, which in its present form began to be generally observed in Britain in the 1950s, has now become a fixed part of the churches' year. It is an occasion for prayer, exchange of pulpits and common worship in many places where nothing else ecumenical ever happens. Sometimes churches will come together for a Bible week or some other similar event.

Even the least of these events require organization and the next normal stage in ecumenical growth is the development of a Clergy and Ministers' Fraternal where the clergy can meet to plan common action. Here very often the ecumenical pattern goes wrong because the clergy, as well as being able to promote ecumenism, are also in a very strong position to prevent it, and this not infrequently happens. If the initial ecumenical events create a great deal of interest then the pressure builds up for something more. Some will wish to create permanent ecumenical machinery and so a council of churches comes into existence. The number of local councils of churches has increased rapidly all over Britain in the last twenty years as the following table shows:

1950	1960	1965	1967	1969
119	300	400	500	650

Since 1969 the growth has been much slower and not a few councils of churches have closed down because they have not seen how to go beyond holding the occasional meeting, organizing Christian Aid Week and observing the Week of Prayer for Christian Unity. In general the effectiveness of a local council of churches is in direct relation to the willingness of the participating congregations to surrender parts of their own life and to commit time and resources to acting ecumenically. These larger cities which employ a full-time secretary for the council of churches have a more active life because the churches have committed money to pay for the full-time officer.

II

The oldest council of churches in Britain is that at Bolton in Lancashire. A series of ecumenical meetings were held in Bolton in 1918 which led to the decision to establish a permanent organization entitled the 'Bolton and District Council of Christian Congregations'. The object of the council was

> to bring nearer the realization of the Kingdom of God by witnessing to, and upholding in all its fullness, the Christian ideal of faith and morals, both in the congregations represented and in the community at large.

At its first meeting letters were read from the secretaries of the Bolton Labour Party and the Bolton Trades' Union Council asking for the churches to send representatives to a conference to discuss the prevention and cure of venereal diseases. The council planned a series of large public meetings dealing with education, work, wages, biblical literature and various aspects of civic life. In the summer they held a series of open-air lectures on the Town Hall steps. The subjects this time were the Bible, Christ's revelation of God, the kingdom of God on earth, womanhood and childhood, marriage and home life, education and leisure, work and wages, and privilege and property. The lectures were all given by local clergy and laymen. The work of the council was in the hands of a small committee and has always had a strong social emphasis. It established a commission for industry and commerce which was a precursor of the present pattern of industrial mission. During the depression in the 1930s it did all it could to help the unemployed and it is at present concerned with vagrancy and teenage drug addiction. It also operates a telephone Samaritan service. There has been little new to report in recent years.

III

In 1940 the first Religion and Life Week was held in Bristol; Bolton had one in 1942 and one was held in Bedford in 1943. Before examining the Bedford Religion and Life Week we must look at the whole concept of Religion and Life Weeks. The idea of these weeks came out of a desire by the churches to communicate to a wider audience the concerns of the 1937 Oxford Conference on Church, Community, and State. This international ecumenical meeting, which was one of the milestones of the ecumenical movement, had convinced many of the need for ecumenical action in relation to social and community affairs. The idea of the weeks was that all the churches in an area would co-operate in a series of meetings and rallies where social concerns could be communicated to a large number of people. Thus a town was 'invaded' by an army of leading ecclesiastical figures to speak at meetings of various sorts. It was a kind of forerunner of PND. There were nine such weeks in 1942, twenty in 1943 and nearly forty in 1944. They led to the formation of many local councils of churches.

In Bedford there was already a Bedford council of Christian churches and in 1942 they agreed to hold a Religion and Life Week in June 1943. This also had support from the Ruridecanal Conference and the Free Church Council, and in addition from the Bedford Hebrew Congregation. Further, the Roman Catholic church agreed to hold a parallel week at the same time under the auspices of 'The Sword of the Spirit'. This body was very influential ecumenically under the leadership of Cardinal Hinsley but ceased to be a strong force in Roman Catholic circles after his death. The preparation for the week was long, careful and not

64

always easy. Some people objected to the involvement of the Roman Catholics and withdrew their support. Nevertheless they had support from the newly formed British Council of Churches and a full programme was finally agreed. Each day of the week had a separate theme and there were several meetings around each theme each day. The themes were as follows:

Monday	The Universal Church and the World Order.
Tuesday	The Home.
Wednesday	Christ and World Peace.
Thursday	Education.
Friday	Commerce, Industry and Agriculture.
Saturday	Youth and Citizenship.

There was united worship on the two Sundays and the final Monday was given over to an analysis of what had happened. The commissions which had been set up to launch the week made recommendations for follow-up work in the town which were very far-reaching and required their continued existence to take these concerns further. It was all very new, never before had the churches co-operated together on such a scale. One who was present commented:

> Surely history was made in Bedford that week. Never before probably, have so many speakers who were acknowledged experts in their subjects been brought into the town within so limited a period. Seldom, if ever, can it have been offered to our citizens to survey the whole field of Christian social action in one comprehensive view. To say that the quality of thought and the standard of eloquence were quite unusual would be to give but a faint idea of the passion that many speakers poured into their utterances . . .

Religion and Life was often described as 'a new form of evangelism'. The chairman of the Bedford week argued that it was essential to bring politics into the pulpit.

> The weakness of the old evangelistic appeal lay in the fact that it was a call to individual salvation out of 'this naughty world'; the challenge of Religion and Life was to a corporate salvation in the

65

midst of society, to share the Cross of Christ amongst those who are being crucified by the conditions of man's livelihood. It was the Challenge of Christ to Society, to citizens and churchmen, in the belief that life could no longer be separated into compartments, 'religious' or 'secular' but was intended by God to become a harmony beneath his all-Sovereign Rule.[1]

As evangelism, Religion and Life Weeks were not an outstanding success. Most of the meetings were attended only by committed Christians. Nevertheless those who went acquired a deeper and wider understanding of the Christian faith. Here was a genuine attempt to relate the gospel to the whole of life and to examine how Christians should participate in society. Looked at from 1971 these weeks do not appear to have radically altered the way Christians behave, but they certainly helped to develop ecumenical partnership and understanding and they helped to put the British Council of Churches on the map.

IV

Welwyn Garden City, one of the first New Towns, was begun in 1920 and a local council of churches was formed there in 1933. Before its establishment there had been some co-operation by the churches in the early years of the town. A United Free Church had been established and the two existing Anglican parishes had another one added to them. During the first ten years Congregational, Methodist, Baptist, Roman Catholic and Quaker congregations were added. The suggestion that there should be a council of churches came out of the need of the Free Churches to form a Free Church Council. They thought that it would be unhelpful to exclude the Anglicans.

The first steps were very tentative. The council thought it would be wise to be simply an advisory rather than an executive body, and to meet only at the request of the members. As confidence grew the council initiated more activities and established a more formal constitution in which the objects of the council were defined as follows:

> To take steps to bring about the co-ordination of Christian witness in the town; to take joint action on agreed matters; to arrange public meetings on religious, social and educational subjects; to endeavour to educate public opinion on special matters and to do all things possible for the deepening of the spiritual life of community.

The activities which expressed these concerns included opposition to a new public house and the provision of accommodation and employment for some of the Jarrow marchers in 1934. The council assisted in resolving the Council tenants' rent strike in 1936. In the post-war period they organized a house-to-house visitation and started a very early shared church (see ch. 5). In 1958 a history was issued to mark the twenty-fifth anniversary, but if you looked at the Welwyn Garden City council of churches today you would find that not much progress had been made; that the same or similar activities continue there and that the expectations put into the objects of the council have not really been fulfilled. One of the largest problems facing local councils of churches is how to move from the period of initial enthusiasm to more creative and permanent expressions of unity.

V

The Scunthorpe council of churches was formed in 1963 following an initiative taken within the clergy fraternal which had been formed in 1959. There was some reluctance from the Anglicans who at that time were busy establishing a group ministry. Nevertheless sufficient impetus was aroused to start the council which then immediately became involved in the plans for the Nottingham Faith and Order Conference. Following that conference and with considerable enthusiasm the council determined to centre its activities on a concern for mission. They launched a programme entitled 'This is our life' in which each denomination demonstrated its own specific witness and belief to others. The main work, however, became more community-centred. They quizzed the candidates for the General Election, small groups were set up to look at specific concerns like education and urban society. The fact that the council had the backing of the long-established industrial mission in Scunthorpe helped considerably.

This programme was followed by PND, which came at the right time and was very well organized. Over 200 people attended the first meeting and two halls had to be used for the closing one. The main recommendations were for the launching of a 'fish scheme', an investigation of the clergy–laity relationship, a worship committee to produce occasional joint services and an education committee to look at Sunday school work. The most significant proposal was for the appointment of an ecumenical development officer who would be appointed for three years to encourage much closer ecumenical growth in the town. His job would be to act as a co-ordinator of all the various groups which were springing up and to help the congregations to move towards a policy of unity in mission.

Two more study programmes followed in the next two years with diminishing effect. The ecumenical development officer, Barrie Hinksman, reports that disillusion set in about the whole operation. He worked as the development officer for over two years and a considerable amount was achieved in terms of raising fundamental questions and bringing the Churches together. His appointment would not have been possible without the financial help of the Anglican diocese and it shows how a church can further ecumenical work if it wishes to do so. Barrie Hinksman's book *Mission and Ministry*[2] provides a valuable case study of the Scunthorpe council of churches. His conclusion, however, is a harshly realistic one. Despite all the effort of a few, little has happened ecumenically in Scunthorpe except the creation of considerable frustration among a large number of lay people. His findings on the role of the council of churches are worth summarizing here.

First, in spite of considerable effort the ecumenical returns have been very small. The weight of tradition and history is against change and is very heavy.

Secondly, the number of people who have an ecumenical vision is in fact extremely small. Moreover, the concept of ecumenism is changing and is now being seen in terms of an open attitude to the whole of life rather than just in terms of the union of churches. Neither of these is seen by the majority of church members as desirable or as a necessary part of the Christian faith.

Thirdly, the council is most effective when it is establishing relationships with the secular. The council of churches is often the only body with whom secular authorities wish to deal. It provides a common point of communication with all the churches.

Fourthly, the council of churches raises in an acute form the question of clergy–laity relationships. While the clergy are dominant in their separate congregations they are much less so in a council of churches. This causes many difficulties. The clergy are in a strong position to criticize lay ideas but less able to provide constructive alternatives. This is the cause of much frustration.

All this leads Hinksman to think that in many ways councils of churches prevent rather than promote ecumenism:

> The present period of apparent paralysis in this council and many like it will not pass until there is a shift in attitudes on the part of the local churches. They are too local, too turned in on themselves and

69

their future, threatened by a feeling that the rest of society is rejecting all that they stand for.[3]

Thus the crisis of ecumenism is really part of the present crisis of the church, and the reason why most local councils of churches are stuck is because the churches are stuck. Barrie Hinksman still thinks that there is a role for the local council but it lies much more in creating attitudes and insights than in promoting a great deal of joint activity.

> Its value lies in a set of attitudes and feelings. It should perhaps consider doing less and less as the executive arm of the churches in that area and simply (not merely) study what is happening in the area awaiting the right moment to respond. The one thing necessary is that the council should develop in itself and in member congregations a *feeling* for what God is doing in his world, as seen in events at local, national and international levels. This feeling is the essence of the ecumenical vision and it needs to be communicated to whomever will listen – in the churches or among the sympathetic public of the district. This communication will be in action when that is called for; in thoughtfully designed acts of worship, few in number, large in size (taking precedence over denominational acts) and lay in character. Above all the present sense of busy-ness with church affairs must be resisted by the council and by constituent congregations.[4]

VI

The creation of right attitudes again seems to be of fundamental importance. It lies behind the work of the Godalming council of churches and it is fundamental to a modern ecumenical spirituality. The four councils of churches here are very similar. Most of them define their objects in a very ambitious way and never fulfil them. They reach a certain point of co-operation and stop there or even fall back from it. The role of the clergy is crucial and in most places they act as an effective brake on further ecumenical growth.

This reveals something about the interim nature of councils of churches. They cannot be regarded as an end in themselves, but only as a means to promote the mission and unity of the church. We have unfortunately reached the stage now where it is considered to be 'respectable' to have a council of churches whether it does anything or not. Thus the country is covered with a network of councils of churches which are tending only to stifle ecumenical growth. The report on *Local Councils of Churches Today* which was presented to the British Council of Churches in 1971 has revealed that the majority of these councils only do two things. One is to observe the Week of Prayer for Christian Unity (and this observance is diminishing). The other is to organize Christian Aid Week (and this function does not require a council of churches as there are nearly 3,000 Christian Aid Week committees and only 700 councils of churches). Unless they can find a new role it is probably better for them to close down.

All this exposes the urgent need for the organic union of the churches. While there are separate denominations, congregations, in order to preserve their own identity, will have to continue a life of their own and will not surrender too much autonomy to others. There is too much history, which is not just local but national, in each denomination and there must be demonstrated a national willingness to surrender inherited autonomy before there can be much ecumenical growth. Whether the type of organic union which we should seek is that which has been envisaged so far is another matter. The growth towards union must take place at every level; without this frustration is inevitable.

Nevertheless there is a role for councils of churches and there are a great many local initiatives which can be taken where people find in themselves a freedom to do so. In the next chapter we shall look at the concept of the ecumenical parish which provides the most local illustration of this. What else is there to be done?

One prerequisite for examining this is to realize that there are different levels of society and therefore different levels at which the church must develop a mission and a strategy. We have seen from Tees-side that a strategy can emerge by differentiating the various levels of society and the levels of church involvement which relate directly to them. The report just mentioned[5] recommended that local councils were *not* needed to promote unity at the local residential level. Here other patterns of ecumenical co-operation were likely to be more viable. The report went on to argue that wherever the churches began to take secular organizations and structures into account an ecumenical approach was a necessity. Borough councils, industry, hospital boards, educational authorities are not really interested in the domestic divisions of Christians. They have a job to do – in which Christians may have a part to play.

The work of councils of churches comes alive when it moves away from its own self-concern and becomes related to secular concerns. This involvement takes two forms. First, the social services and many other agencies are manned to a considerable extent by committed Christians who in their individual capacities are providing many services to the community. Secondly, there are the opportunities open to a council of churches to act on behalf of the churches over a matter of common concern to church and state. We have seen this in every local council which we have looked at. Too often these activities have been sporadic and have taken the form of protesting about something rather than sharing in some creative activity. Why should there not be much more regular and frequent contact by the churches with all levels of society? In this way the church can contribute to concern about the total quality of life in an area. Concern for education can express itself in providing a meeting place for teachers who wish to examine fundamental issues. Clergy and doctors can meet together to examine their understanding of the nature of healing. In many areas Christians will wish to raise fundamental questions about the presuppositions about man which are being used by planners, the leisure industry and so on. Thus opportunities will emerge for evangelism, pastoral care, dialogue and many other aspects of the Christian mission. This approach may demand that the church plays a prophetic and political role when injustice or narrow self-interest is seen to be motivating some social action. It is at the borough, county or regional level that a council of churches may contribute to the mission of God.

A council of churches also has a role in relation to the churches' self-understanding. As a body, with an ecclesial nature but slightly outside congregational and denominational life, it may help through surveys, the use of theological experts and study groups, to enable the churches to see their own position more clearly and help them to use their own resources more wisely in terms of the priorities for mission.

Moreover the council of churches can be a valuable means of communication between the churches and on behalf of the churches. We have seen how the Godalming council of churches through its magazine *Link* gives a common means of communication to all the churches there. The use of a magazine has been adopted elsewhere as well. A person who will spend considerable time on direct face to face communication can make all the difference to the effectiveness or otherwise of a council of churches.

The use of the local press can also be helpful especially if it is used in an imaginative way. It can provide the basis for helping people to do theology for themselves. The development of local radio is even more important and councils of churches have been very quick to see the advantage of this and are using local radio programmes very fully. Even more, however, could be done; it might be possible for example, for a study programme for ecumenical groups to use local radio as its main means of communication.

In the age of the mass media Christians must learn together how to communicate the gospel through the media. If we cannot communicate the gospel effectively there is a strong probability that we do not believe it ourselves. Some councils of churches have tried to grapple with the means of communicating faith today and Sheffield has developed a creative programme on the meaning of personal witness today. This has consisted of groups of people with various outlooks going away for a weekend together to examine what each of them understood about Christian faith and experience, then going on to see how they could communicate this in various life situations. Here we can see the value of conference centres and places like Scottish Churches House, Dunblane, which can be used by councils of churches and others to take people apart to examine issues in depth. Such groups need not necessarily be entirely Christian. It is in encounters like this that many will find out what they really believe.

But as soon as activities start to be listed we are back at the question of whether individual congregations and members are prepared to support ecumenical activity. Many of them are not. It is partly for this reason that the BCC report suggests that councils of churches should not exist at the neighbourhood level but at town and borough level and that representation on them should be through *denominations* and not from congregations. At the neighbourhood level whole congregations should try to work together directly and not through a representative body. At a higher level, especially when money and manpower may be needed, denominational representation becomes important. This is also the case when strong links are being established with the secular, which requires a denominational rather than a congregational presence.

74

Somehow the desire for unity in mission has to be created in the churches; this may be easier through specific projects than through an overall policy. While congregations may not in general be willing to contribute considerable resources to the activities of councils of churches, they may be willing to contribute manpower or resources for a project which they see is worthwhile. Or one congregation may be prepared to act on behalf of others where they obviously have the right expertise. In this way, and through occasional acts of common prayer and worship a confidence in each other may grow which will enable more people to see the need for unity.

In the main, councils of churches have engaged in activities which could easily be done together and which would not produce too much conflict. When conflict has arisen they have usually run away from it. Councils have avoided the difficult things and this is why they are frustrated. Conflict can be creative and should not be avoided. Very few councils of churches take a serious and active part in theological debate. Almost none have taken any note of the church union negotiations taking place in their member churches. Very few councils have ever seriously challenged the autonomy of their participating congregations. All this and much more must happen if the council is to be a live body. There must not be a fear of conflict but an awareness that through conflict comes strength and conviction. If an ecumenical body cannot cope with differences of opinion it is hard to see what kind of unity it has. Surely Christian love and forgiveness are meant to overcome disagreement and at the heart of unity lies a willingness to accept those with whom you disagree? It is out of this creative conflict that a real understanding of unity will emerge which is not static but dynamic, not uniform but diverse.

NOTES

1. These quotations are from the report of the Bedford Religion and Life Week, privately printed by the Bedford Council of Christian Congregations in 1943.

2. B. Hinksman, *Mission and Ministry*, 1970, available from the British Council of Churches.

3. *Op. cit.*, p.21.

4. *Ibid*.

5. *Local Councils of Churches Today*, British Council of Churches 1971.

5 The Ecumenical Parish

Among other resolutions the Nottingham Faith and Order Conference called on the churches to:

> . . . designate areas of ecumenical experiment, at the request of local congregations, or in new towns and housing areas. In such areas there should be experiments in ecumenical group ministries, in the sharing of buildings and equipment, and in the development of mission.[1]

The conference's 'Section on Ministry' expanded what it meant by this in the following words:

> Some experiments are already in being in the field of *group ministry* (an ecumenical group of ordained men) and of *team ministry* (a group of full-time workers, ordained and non-ordained, men and women, which might be denominational or ecumenical). Many more are required to provide a new, common strategy in downtown areas and on new estates, with the co-operation of several churches. The necessity of appointing the right men in such 'areas of ecumenical experiment' might mean new machinery of appointment. Not only should there be a joint policy on the use of church buildings; it would also be good, in a new area, to experiment without definite church buildings in group ministry, to gather, nourish and send out a Christian community.[2]

These comments were not just based on theory. Behind them lay the experience of a few places which had already been working along these lines and the vision of others who saw possibilities in the concept of 'ecumenical experiment'.

The first place which might be called an area of ecumenical experiment in Britain was the Redfield United Front in Bristol. This was started by Mervyn Stockwood, now

Bishop of Southwark, when he was vicar of St Matthew Moorfields, Bristol. During the height of the enemy bombing on Bristol he called together the clergy of all denominations in the Redfield area to see what could be done together. This led into a pattern of joint co-operation, intercommunion, shared work and worship throughout the area. This was in many ways a major breakthrough and its activities took the whole of society into account and therefore included considerable political activity.

In Welwyn Garden City a new area was established in the post-war period. The local council of churches opened up negotiations with the Development Corporation about the new area of Ludwick. This negotiation led to the establishment of the Ludwick Family Club and Church. This was a dual-purpose hall, part of which was set apart as a church chancel and sanctuary. The hall was used for community activities during the week and for church worship on Sundays. An Anglican curate was appointed to look after the area, not just for the Anglicans but on behalf of all the member churches of the council. This project began in 1949 and went on for seven years. But all was not well. It is not clear from the records what went wrong, but in 1956 the curate made the following statement to the council of churches executive committee:

> During the last few months, I have come to the conclusion that the experiment in church co-operation at Ludwick should be drastically curtailed. In the past we have maintained that the witness of the church is more effective where Christians are united. This is true in the social, moral and ethical sphere, but probably not true in the building up of a local church in a new district . . . In a new area . . . displaced persons must grow new roots and this they do most strongly in ways which are familiar to them and in the company of likeminded people. Newcomers to the district who are already churchgoers want to go where services are familiar and where they feel at home.[3]

So the Ludwick experiment came to an end. The reasons given for ending it are very confused. What people have in common in a new area is that they are all new; the church is not likely to make all that amount of difference. There seems to be a suggestion in this statement of the needs of the minister to have an identifiable group around him and the needs of some to cling to a nostalgic view of the congregation which they have left. Above all this statement reveals a lack of sense of mission. It is not after all the church community which matters, but the total community in the area, and the lack of willingness to assist the community comes over very strongly. We see here some of the tensions which lie behind the concept of an ecumenical experiment. Another new area of Welwyn Garden City is being developed at the present time and the churches are again planning an ecumenical approach. It is to be hoped that this does not suffer the same fate.

It was in the 1960s that the idea of new experiments in mission really began to take shape. There were several reasons for this. The early 1960s were a time of growing confidence among the churches and there was a willingness to co-operate with others. Also union schemes were under discussion and had not yet reached the point of decision and subsequent disillusion. This confidence faded as the decade progressed, but its ecumenical confidence was revealed at its fullest in the Nottingham Faith and Order Conference.

There was also a growing concern for the mission of the church. An awareness of the introverted nature of much church life was leading many to think again about mission. We have already referred to the influence of the WCC study on the missionary structure of the congregation, *The Church for Others*. This encouraged many to try and find new forms of mission and ministry. The great difficulties of changing the institutional structures had not yet become apparent. Related to this was the growing dissatisfaction among the younger clergy with the normal pattern of pastoral ministry.

79

This expressed itself in the activities of the renewal groups and in the reluctance of many to enter into traditional pastoral work. It seemed to them that what might have been a suitable pattern in the pre-industrial age had now become impossible to operate in terms of the life style of contemporary man. The pioneering work of industrial mission and other new forms of ministry had shown that there might be other ways forward. The church had become part of the social life of the middle-class, nearly everywhere else very little was happening. The frustration was particularly clear to those working in New Towns and housing estates where the churches had assumed that the traditional pattern would still work. This had led to a great waste of expenditure on buildings and plant in new areas. For instance the Anglicans had built three new churches in Corby at a cost of £1,000,000. By 1970 these were running at a deficit of over £20,000 a year and the normal churchgoing population was about 250. This could easily have been housed in one of the churches.[4]

Moreover, Britain is undergoing a rapid social change. The population is increasing at a rate of over 3,000,000 every ten years. Twenty-one New Towns have been built and possibly as many again are on the way. The population of the existing New Towns will be over two and a half million by the end of the century. In addition many existing large towns are being doubled in size. Nearly eighty proposals for such expansion have already been agreed (in places like Northampton, Warrington, Aylesbury, Kings Lynn, as well as in the large conurbations like London, Liverpool, Manchester and Birmingham). The number of new development schemes approved each year is about twelve and this number is likely to increase. In terms of housing alone it is not simply a matter of houses for new families but the re-housing of families moved as a result of slum clearance. Moreover, modern patterns of industry and employment are making the population much more mobile and so the style of life of people is changing considerably. There is much bewilderment in the lives of people and a need to find new roles and a new identity within the new areas. All this requires that the church considers very carefully how it is to serve the gospel in this kind of society. It is a time for experiment.

In other parts of the world the churches are making experiments under similar conditions. In Australia the Belconnen area of Canberra is being operated by five denominations acting together. These are the Anglicans, Churches of Christ, Congregationalists, Methodists and Presbyterians. There is also growing co-operation with the Roman Catholics. Belconnen is a regional town adjacent to Canberra which is planned to have a population of 120,000 people. The planners want it to be an entity in itself providing all the main facilities for living (education, employment, shopping, culture, entertainment, commerce, etc.). The town will consist of twenty-six residential units and later a town centre. The churches are planning to relate their main activities to the neighbourhood centres. In these they are intending to place clergy houses and demountable buildings for church gatherings. When the centre is built it is proposed to establish a complex of meeting rooms, offices, etc. which will be the focal point of the churches' mission to the central town structures. Roman Catholic involvement is expected in this centre. There is to be a team approach to the total area whereby the clergy and some lay people will exercise specialist ministries in relation to various aspects of town life. The whole project is to be governed by a leaders' council which will relate to the denominations and a number of group councils covering several neighbourhoods.

This type of project is being adopted in places other than Britain and Australia. Rüdiger Reitz in his book *The Church in Experiment*[5] describes several similar attempts in the

United States where churches in an existing town have pooled their resources to make better use of them in terms of a total mission to the area. Thus the Philadelphia Co-operative Ministry was a merger of four congregations in which one pastor was given overall control of the project and a co-operative council established. All programmes for the area are agreed by the council while at the same time each congregation has its own life. A director of Christian education works in all four congregations. It seems as if in some areas this kind of approach will be the only way forward. The only alternative is for small congregations just to get smaller and die away.

The Nottingham Conference resolution sparked off considerable activity in various parts of Britain and a survey conducted in 1967 revealed that there were about 200 places where ecumenical co-operation had gone well beyond the level of normal activity through local councils of churches.[6] But it was also clear that the phrase 'area of ecumenical experiment' lacked proper definition. There were shared buildings, ecumenical team ministries and places where they had called themselves 'areas of ecumenical experiment' simply to get round existing ecclesiastical discipline. One of the more developed situations was at Blackbird Leys, Oxford, where a new area which had originally been operated only by the Church of England was able to form an ecumenical ministry sharing one church building. This happened because the Congregational church sold one of its buildings and was able to put some money into providing a man and a house. All the Free Churches in Oxford contributed to his salary and two men have worked together ever since. For part of the time they had a woman church worker with them as well. The Bishop of Oxford was not willing to allow intercommunion to take place and therefore there had to be separate Sunday morning worship. In fact this meant that those who attended worship went to whatever service suited them regardless of denomination while the ministers kept their denominational services going! The clergy spent a great deal of their time involved in community projects and increasingly found that the Anglican church, which had been designed only for worship, was an embarrassment to them. Blackbird Leys is not an area of ecumenical experiment but it could become one.

Some of the most thorough thinking about the nature of an ecumenical experiment was done in Northamptonshire by a group which produced a document entitled *Planning the Ecumenical Parish*.[7] It spelled out in detail how an ecumenical parish might be established. In particular it contained key ideas which have been a major contribution to all subsequent thinking on this subject. The first of these was the need to see that the area of the experiment was properly defined. An experiment, they argued, must be conducted under careful conditions in a properly defined area. Within this area it is necessary for at least some, if not all denominational traditions to be suspended for a period. This is inherent in the concept of the ecumenical nature of the experiment. Thus they wrote:

It rapidly became obvious to us that this [an ecumenical parish] was not possible unless, for the sake of the experiment, we were all prepared to lay aside some of our more strongly held denominational convictions and accept the validity of each other's claims to be part of the church. This we have done as the only alternative to saying either that the task was impossible, or that it could produce so little by way of positive suggestion to be valueless.

Thus we see here a strong plea for a new attitude to ecumenical work. Unless there is a real willingness to surrender things which we think are important very little can happen. Moreover by being willing to surrender them in a experimental situation we shall be able to test whether they are so central to our Christian faith as we thought. In many cases we shall find that they are not and our acceptance of others will be greatly increased. The report then suggests that this suspension of denominational traditions would only be practicable in new areas. As we shall see, this has not proved to be the case.

The other main contribution from the document was the concept of the 'sponsoring body'. They saw the need for a body which would sponsor the experiment and also be the point at which the participating denominations could be represented in relation to the experiment. The sponsoring body would thus act as a 'buffer' between the experiment and the churches. The sponsoring body would be responsible for all finance and policy, but as it would consist of representatives of existing denominations there was little danger of a new denomination coming into existence.

The need for a closer definition of an 'area of ecumenical experiment' became clear as a result of this initial survey. Following the failure of the Anglican Church to obtain the necessary majority to achieve union with the Methodists in 1969, some local churches wanted to unite locally, and a few did so. The term 'area of ecumenical experiment' was in danger of becoming a cover for rejecting church discipline. Thus in 1969 the Department of Mission and Unity of the British Council of Churches convened a meeting to provide a closer definition. This meeting, attended by those engaged in experiments together with some church dignitaries and ecclesiastical lawyers, has produced a document which is now being used as the basis for areas of experiment. Also during 1969 the Sharing of Church Buildings Act 1969 received the Royal Assent. This act resolved most of the legal difficulties which had previously surrounded the sharing of church buildings by members of different denominations. This almost certainly means that the majority of new church buildings will be shared ones.

The BCC document begins by defining the different levels of ecumenical co-operation. The first level is that of co-operation through local councils of churches. We have already seen what are the difficulties of local councils of churches. The second level is that of an area of ecumenical co-operation. This is defined as follows:

> Areas where, within the limits of existing denominational traditions, there is a very considerable degree of co-operation between the churches of an area in their mission to the people and in the common life of these congregations.[8]

Thus an area of co-operation goes as far as existing denominational discipline will allow. But that can be quite a long way. What is envisaged is a procedure whereby congregations in a defined area come together to discuss what activities they are going to share together. When certain proposals have been agreed in detail by the decision-making bodies in each congregation, an act of covenant or commitment to God and each other should be held, involving all the participating congregations. Such an act might be repeated annually as new pieces of co-operation are undertaken. There is no limit to the kind of activities which might take place. There could be shared worship, joint youth work and Sunday schools, common visitation of new areas, joint newspapers or magazines and many other things. What is important about this concept is that it allows a continued policy to develop and is not so dependent upon the wills or wishes of the clergy.

The third level which overlaps with the second and the fourth is that of shared church buildings. The fourth is the area of ecumenical experiment. The BCC document describes them as:

> Areas where, under responsible authority, certain denominational traditions are suspended for a period in order that new patterns of worship, mission and ministry can be undertaken. Evaluation of such experiments is an essential part of the project.

The document then goes on to give details of how the area may be set up. The definition is the key to the whole document. The main points are the limited area of the experiment and the fact that because it is an experiment it cannot go on for ever and it must be properly assessed. It is also implicit in the concept of an experiment that those who enter into the experiment do not know what they are going to discover, but are willing to learn and to test out certain ideas. So far it is at this point that many experiments are still not too clear. Many of them are simply Christians from different traditions doing together the same things that they were originally doing separately, and that is not much of an experiment.

The key to the experiment is the sponsoring body and its work is defined as follows:

(a) To establish the experiment.
(b) To approve and make appointments to the team(s).
(c) To provide for negotiation over matters of planning to be undertaken with the secular and ecclesiastical authorities.
(d) To negotiate with the participating denominations their financial contributions, and to obtain additional finances to meet the costs of running the experiment.
(e) Where shared buildings are involved, to ensure that the requirements of the Sharing of Church Buildings Act 1969 are met.
(f) To be available to give guidance in legal, theological and disciplinary matters.
(g) To act in a consultative role to the team.
(h) To promote understanding of experiments amongst the participating denominations and to provide regular written reports.

The way in which this is working out in practice is that some sponsoring bodies are responsible for a single area, but there are also places, such as Bristol, where a sponsoring body has been set up which will act on behalf of several experiments.

It is very important that every experiment should be properly assessed. The period of the experiment is expected to be about seven years but the assessment must be an ongoing process which continues all the time. At the end of seven years the experiment will cease. This does not mean that the situation will revert to what it was before. That would be impossible. It simply means that the situation will either become regularized or that some parts of the experiment will be dropped and others carried on. We need to remember that experiments cannot fail; they can only test out ideas and provide us with new approaches to mission.

The first area in England to be officially designated was Desborough in Northamptonshire. This town of 5,000 population has gradually moved towards this position over the last twenty years. A council of churches was formed in 1953. In 1965 a joint mission was held in the town and this was followed by an investigation into the Nottingham resolution on ecumenical experiments. The congregations (Anglican, Methodist, Baptist and Congregationalist) all agreed unanimously to be designated as an area of experiment. They saw three advantages in this:

> First we would be able to advance towards full union ahead of the main stream of our denominations and so make available to the church as a whole the fruits of our experience.
> Secondly it was felt that it would be easier for the Bishop of the Anglican Church and the Chairman of the Methodist District to allow experiments to be worked out within a designated area, for which they might be unwilling to grant universal permission.
> Thirdly it was felt that it would ensure a continuity of emphasis despite the inevitable changes in the ministers who serve here.[9]

Following this a joint governing body was set up which was given considerable power to make decisions by the four churches. This body issued a declaration of intent, which included these words:

> ... we believe that a united church in Desborough is inevitable because we cannot forever frustrate the will of God and yet although we passionately desire to be obedient to God and long for unity in

Christ, we recognize that there are still many factors, theological and traditional, great and small, which must be resolved before we enter upon such a union. We believe that only by careful study, prayer, and preparation together can we avoid a repetition of the sins of the past. But also we believe that this work of preparation for reunion can be carried out only within the context of mutual trust and commitment to the common goal of ultimate organic union.[10]

In the light of this they set up nine working commissions to examine every area of the churches' life in Desborough and made recommendations as to how they could be brought together. At this point the Baptist and Congregationalist ministers left the area and both churches were without ministers for some time. In the meanwhile the Anglicans and the Methodists went ahead. This led to a common declaration by the Desborough Parochial Church Council and the Trustees of Desborough Methodist Church which recommended that they should now become one church. To enable this to happen it was agreed that the Anglican parish church should be the centre for worship and that the Methodist property should be sold. A new hall for educational work was to be built, the cost of which should be shared. An order for Sunday worship was agreed and it was agreed to seek for full intercommunion from the very beginning. There would be both Anglican and Methodist communion services but they would be open to all. There would be a team ministry and subsequent appointments would be made after careful consultation. This plan was agreed in September 1968, and on 7 September 1969 the experiment was formally inaugurated at a service conducted jointly by the Chairman of the Methodist District and the Bishop of Peterborough. It had taken a long time to come to fruition, but people had been fully consulted at every point. This is an essential part of such a project.

There are now nearly thirty designated areas of ecumenical experiment and others are being negotiated. There is also a much larger number of shared churches. Roman Catholic involvement in shared buildings is not so great but it already exists in about twenty places. At Cippenham in Slough a new joint Anglican/Roman Catholic church was established in 1970. Others are being planned. At Livingston in Scotland the New Town is being tackled by an ecumenical team, but the participating denominations are each being responsible for one church building. Here also there is a pattern of reciprocal intercommunion. Thus very gradually new patterns of pastoral strategy are being evolved.

But this brings us to a paradoxical matter. The areas of ecumenical experiment are in pastoral, parochial situations. This is because all the churches in Britain have seen the mission of the church almost entirely in terms of the mission to the residential area. There are good historical reasons for this. The church had seen itself as relating to the area where most people lived most of their lives and this is what the parish used to be. The whole weight of history lies in the pastoral and parochial ministry. It is here that there are legal provisions and regulations. It is here that there are denominational traditions, customs and disciplines which have to be questioned and experimented with. If the church wishes to experiment with mission in relation to industry, leisure or commerce, or to establish a proper role in relation to decision-making and planning, then there is no need to establish an area of ecumenical experiment because there are no traditions to be suspended and no precedents to be observed.

The question also has to be raised about the relation between the ecumenical parish and organic union. The declaration of intent from Desborough made it quite clear that they did not see that what they were doing was in any way a substitute for organic union. Ecumenical experiments result in the need for organic union being more clearly seen. This is partly because an overall policy and strategy cannot be organized locally, but also because there are intractable problems which must be resolved at a national level. The chief of these is the matter of church membership. Most people in an ecumenical experiment already belong to one or other of the participating denominations, but what happens to those who join the church for the first time in this ecumenical setting? At the moment there is agreement that they must join a denomination at some point either when they join the church or when they move away from the ecumenical area. But this problem will only be properly resolved when the churches have become one. The experiment heightens the anomaly of Christian division.

At the same time there are those who have argued that local union will be the way to achieve organic union. The authors of *Growing into Union*,[11] who include J. I. Packer and the Bishop of Willesden, have proposed that a united church should be achieved by local churches entering into union so that gradually a united church is achieved from the bottom up. This proposal is open to question on many fronts, not least because it lacks a proper theology of mission. It assumes, once again, that the present parochial pattern for mission is sufficient. It does not consider how mission is to be achieved in relation to other areas of society. For instance the authors are a little confused about the role of cathedrals, which do not fit into their pattern. They do not seem to see the essentially diverse nature which the church must have in today's complex society.

There is a real interaction between areas of experiment and the search for Christian unity. For the unity which we seek must be a unity which will communicate the gospel of Christ to the world today. The point of the experiment is to discover new patterns of mission and ministry, to discover what should be the shape of the church in this age. Experi-

90

ment is therefore a complement to the search for organic unity. P. R. Clifford is surely right when he comments:

> The fact remains that the success or failure of [union] schemes depends on the way in which churches are prepared to co-operate locally in ministry and mission.[12]

He then goes on to argue that one of the virtues of making experiments is that it enables the church to try out new approaches without abandoning the present *modus vivendi*. He calls on the churches to put more resources into experiments in the hope that from them new patterns will emerge which will be acceptable and serve the needs of mission today. The fact that the idea of ecumenical experiment is gradually gaining acceptance in the churches may well be a sign that they are moving towards willingness for organic unity. But there needs to be much more support than there has been so far if this is to be significant.

One of the hindrances to experiment is that people object to being experimented upon. They feel this is an intrusion into their ecclesiastical life. This points us again to the attitude of mind which is necessary for ecumenical work. People are not being experimented upon – they are the experimenters. There is a great need for people to understand experimentation as a proper Christian function and one which can be understood as such. Thus Rüdiger Reitz sees experimentation as being a necessary function of the church in a revolutionary age:

> Unfortunately the bias against the word *experiment* is still considerable among many theologians and church members. But experiment in the church no longer proves to be something provisional in a negative sense. It has become a structural imperative . . . A look at the constructive unrest in the church makes us ask if *vita experimentalis* is not the contribution of God's wandering people for the last third of this century.[13]

If this is the case then we are moving into a phase where we shall need to have an experimental theology as the basis of our experimental life. Hans Hoekendijk has made some tentative comments on this. He sees experimental theology as one in which the received tradition is tested against the action of today in the hope that new truths may emerge. Old truth is already part of the tradition. Mission may be seen as the action by which we test tradition in experiment. Thus he sees an experimental theology emerging in contrast to both propositional theology and traditional theology. By means of experiment we can find out what happens to tradition and also what emerges as a new tradition. In doing this we are not just dealing with doctrine but risking ourselves for the sake of the gospel. Experiment has always been an essential part of mission. For instance the admission of the Gentiles into the early church was a very bold experiment, which clearly involved great risks and for which there was no precedent.

David Jenkins in his Bampton lectures[14] takes this concept of experiment even further. He sees life as an experiment whereby we seek new truths and then apply them in order to find new truths and new meanings. This is a continuous process which he also sees in God himself. Thus he interprets the incarnation as God's experiment in becoming man and so gives us the justification to see life in this same way. God is the experimenter, man is to follow him in experimenting with life. The church must be an experimental institution if it is to follow in the footsteps of Jesus Christ our forerunner who blazes the trail to God for us.

The ecumenical parish is one expression of this experimental life which the church must follow in the world today.

NOTES

1. D. L. Edwards and R. E. Davies, *Unity Begins at Home*, SCM Press 1964, p.79.
2. *Ibid.*, p.69.

3. F. M. Page, *Some Notes on the Life of the Church in Welwyn Garden City*, printed for private circulation, 1958, p.24.

4. *The Church in Corby – a report from the Anglican Clergy*. Issued January 1971. The figures quoted here do not include clergy salaries.

5. R. Reitz, *The Church in Experiment*, Abingdon Press, USA, 1969.

6. R. M. C. Jeffery, *Areas of Ecumenical Experiment*, BCC 1968.

7. *Ibid.*, Appendix A.

8. For the complete document, see R. M. C. Jeffery, *Ecumenical Experiments – A Handbook*, BCC 1971.

9. *Areas of Ecumenical Experiment*, p.9.

10. *Ibid.*, p.10.

11. The Bishop of Willesden and others, *Growing into Union*, SPCK 1970.

12. P. R. Clifford, *Now is the Time*, Collins 1970, p.67.

13. *The Church in Experiment*, pp.188–9.

14. D. Jenkins, *The Glory of Man*, SCM Press 1968.

6 Planning for Mission

I

Traditionally there have been two missionary methods used in Britain; there has been the parish (local based) ministry, and the evangelistic preaching mission. Historically the preaching mission often emerged out of a dissatisfaction with the parish ministry. This is how the friars and other preaching orders began their work. It was the way in which the evangelical revival in England in the eighteenth century was established. Wesley and Whitefield did not reject the local-based ministry, but they found it inadequate as a means of communicating the gospel, so they travelled the country preaching where they could and establishing 'societies' to carry on their work. It has been maintained by some that this preaching saved England from a revolution like that of France. Others, notably E. P. Thompson,[1] argue that Methodism was an effective tool for suppressing the working classes, and there is probably more truth in that than many would care to admit. This debate need not concern us now. What the debate reveals is that the evangelical preachers were as much conditioned by the social climate of their day as anyone else. It is doubtful whether the gospel can ever be extracted from the culture in which it is preached, and this raises great problems for us today. It certainly means that we must understand our own society as fully as possible. We see the substitution of mass evangelism for the pastoral ministry today in the Billy Graham campaigns and in the work of such bodies as the Faith Mission whose activities in the Hebrides during the 1950s have been usefully documented recently.[2]

Whatever the advantages of these two methods of mission, they are both now under question from many sources. In the Church of England the reform of the parochial ministry is under active consideration in such legislation as the Pastoral Measure and in the many proposals on the deployment of the clergy which so far have not been implemented. The report on Mission presented to the General Assembly of the Church of Scotland in May 1971[3] also attacked the narrow parochialism of the Kirk and called for the establishment of group ministries relating to the whole of society. The local ministry has its critics in all churches because it seems to have degenerated into being the servicing of a religious club.

Evangelistic campaigns are being questioned by many because they are so often just 'preaching to the converted'. The Evangelical Alliance report *On the Other Side* questions the use of mass evangelism and of the concentration of effort on teenagers. Another book by a member of the team which produced that report, Gavin Reid, entitled *The Gagging of God*,[4] demonstrates the inability of the church to communicate the gospel in the age of the mass media.

It might be helpful to go behind these missionary methods to the concerns which they exemplify and see whether there may not be better means of achieving their desired ends. The parish ministry sprang out of a concern for a total mission to the whole community. Originally the parish was the place where most people lived most of their lives. Lesslie Newbigin makes the point well when he writes:

> When the barbarian tribes accepted the Christian faith under the leadership of their chiefs and were baptized *en masse*, what was needed was a place in each community where the whole population could gather together for worship and instruction in the new faith. There had to be a church building in the centre of each town or

95

village. The visible centre of the church's life became a place which truly expressed the divine invitation 'Come unto me', but which could not in the same sense express the divine command 'Go – and I am with you'. There was nowhere to go.[5]

This was how the parish ministry began. It was related to the whole community which was already Christian. It concerned itself with every aspect of the life of man. The local ecclesiastical parish is no longer such a place. The area in which most men live most of their lives is much wider. While there will certainly be a place for the neighbourhood ministry, it can no longer claim to be the only ministry but a specialist ministry among others.

The evangelistic campaign has always been concerned with the effective communication of the gospel and the encouragement of personal commitment to Christ. It often had appended to it certain specific theological presuppositions and dogmatic assumptions, but as not all the preaching missions shared the same ones (contrast for instance Wesley and Whitefield), this need not concern us here.

Behind these missionary methods are three basic concerns: a total ministry to the whole community, effective communication of the gospel and personal commitment to Christ. These three factors are interdependent – the first would mean very little without the other two. The question of contemporary spirituality has already been examined in chapter 2. It must be open and take the world seriously. When we have a Christian style of life which makes sense then modern man will be interested in why we have it.

In terms of effective communication Christians have much to learn about the advantages and the limitations of the use of the mass media. It will not solve all our problems, but there is much that it can teach us. One of the most effective means of communication comes out of the valuable work which is actually being done. There is not much to be said for those, and they are many, who are so busy telling people

96

what they are doing that they are in fact doing nothing at all.

This chapter is concerned with attempts by the churches to exercise a total ministry to the whole community. To discover how this is to be done requires a careful examination of the way our society is being structured and moulded. We are still not doing enough about this. We shall see later how the failure to appreciate planning procedures has militated against effective mission in New Towns. Patterns of education are forming new types of character; scientific developments and cultural patterns are deeply affecting the way we live. Unless the church is actively involved and concerned in these matters it is unlikely that it will be able to make the gospel relevant to our own society.

Over the past ten years Britain has been moving towards a regional approach to the organization of its life. The first expression of this were the Economic Planning Councils whose reports have provided considerable data on the regions and plans for their future development. The London boroughs have been reorganized and following the Maud and Wheatley reports the reorganization of the rest of local government is imminent. These new areas will be much more like the area in which most people live most of their lives. The region is the area where people not only have their homes but also their work, their leisure and their education. The region is in some sense what the parish used to be. So churches need to take the region more seriously. The Yorkshire Churches Group has been raising the question of the role of the church in the region. In Tees-side they are attempting to establish a total mission there (see ch. 1).

How is this to be worked out by those who wish to follow this pattern? Tees-side would not claim that what they are doing is a blueprint for everywhere else. The churches in each area will have to do their own groundwork and theological analysis to see how this might work out. We shall look at an actual situation where this process is going on and which we shall call Breadhurst.

This is a large town in the south of England which is a communications centre for road and rail and has been a transport centre for centuries. It has become an industrial centre and is in the process of having its population trebled. The population has been moving in chiefly from London. The old town centre is being developed to be the centre of this whole area. The church in Breadhurst consists of an ancient Anglican parish church with three daughter churches and two other Anglican parishes. Both of the latter are rather evangelical – unlike the old parish church. There are two Methodist churches, a Baptist and a Congregationalist church and two Roman Catholic churches which are operated by a team of priests.

The new areas which are being built around the town are being tackled in various ways by the churches. Two areas are being operated ecumenically and one may well become an area of ecumenical experiment. With all this already existing the churches together have to decide how to respond to the changing pattern of society which is developing around them. How can they find effective patterns of mission within this complex society? Already in Breadhurst there is a variety of approaches to the residential ministry; why not take this variety further and by experimentation and assessment find out what are the effective patterns for the area? The test of effectiveness must also be established and this will be a subject of much theological debate along the lines illustrated in chapter 3 of this book. But one of the ways of resolving this debate is to test one mission strategy based on one principle against another based on a different one. The following patterns would seem to be possible ones:

1. A conservative evangelical approach centring round the preaching of the Word and Bible study and prayer groups.

2. A sacramental approach centred around frequent eucharists and house communions.
3. A multi-denominational approach with several churches offering different traditions to the neighbourhood.
4. Ecumenical areas where the churches co-operate fully.
5. Areas of ecumenical experiment as outlined in the previous chapter.
6. Common sharing of a single church. This could be part of an area of ecumenical experiment; it could also be a separate project.
7. Operating an area without any building at all to see how the church evolves itself.

Within all these projects various other methods and techniques could be used for the communication and working out of the gospel. One area could be concerned with the use of the insights gained from the work of sensitivity training and group activity. This might be related to the use of community development techniques which are well suited to the church. Another area might centre its concerns on techniques of social action, based on the assumption that the gospel must express itself in social change. There is a considerable amount of expertise which has been built up on this basis from America, though it needs very careful handling to relate to the British scene. We do not live under such strong social pressures as they do.

Another area might concentrate on the type of evangelistic techniques described in *On the Other Side* which are summed up in the phrase 'evangelism in depth'. Another area might explore the use of techniques which might commend themselves more to the less literate members of the population. This would include the use of movement, drama, role play, painting and modelling and aspects of non-verbal communication. Yet another area might see its main concern as full co-operation with the secular authorities and work towards the type of activity already described from Tees-side.

If these were all used side-by-side, it would be possible to assess their relative value, and the presuppositions which lie behind them. The material for a proper theological investigation of the role of the church today will emerge in this way.

Breadhurst needs to be looked at as a whole, and the church needs to see its role in relation to the main social structures. There is for instance a considerable amount of industry and a strong case can be made out for the development of industrial mission especially in relation to commerce and transport. The need for the Christian ministry in this area is now generally understood, but the methods which it involves are less well appreciated. Industrial mission in Britain has been going through a difficult time, but there is sufficient expertise available to make possible a better understanding of its potentialities. Thus through contact with management and workers, conferences and study groups, and work with individuals the church can help forward a careful examination of the attitudes and philosophy of industry which moulds so much of modern man's life.

Then in relation to educational facilities the churches need to have a common strategy, not only in relation to church schools but in relation to the whole field of educational facilities.

There is a large hospital in Breadhurst. There is also a full-time hospital chaplain. This can provide the basis for an area of mission which is concerned not simply with the care of the sick but with the nature of the total community and the way in which a healthy society can be developed. Michael Wilson has recently made clear the significance of this in his book *The Hospital – a Place of Truth*.[6] Related to this is the provision of the social services, and here Breadhurst would do well to take a leaf out of the book of the Maidstone council of churches, which in 1964 with the co-operation and support of the local Council carried out a survey of the whole area with a view to examining exactly what were the provisions of the social services and what gaps existed. This survey, *Maidstone – a Closer Look*,[7] led to the establishment to the Maidstone Council of Social Service and the provision of much more voluntary service in the area.

The central town churches of Breadhurst have a very specific function to fulfil in relation to the political structures of the area, the planning authorities and similar bodies. They can provide a centre for mid-week meetings, be used as places for experimental worship and provide links with the local press and other parts of the communications media. Perhaps their most essential function will be to act as a training centre for Christians in the whole area. People from all over the town find it easy to come to the centre. Central churches can be used for lectures, group work and weekend courses to enable people to become more articulate about their faith. One approach which they might consider is something that so far has not been done in Britain. This is the idea of 'Town Talk' which was launched in Lakehead City in Canada in 1967.[8] Town Talk is a method evolved for ensuring a strong community sense throughout the whole area and enabling real participation by the majority of people. The centre of it is a one-month blitz on the town following a two-year period of preparation. Louis Wilson describes Town Talk as:

discussion – action on social issues;

a methodology for total community involvement and action on key issues;

a community-wide saturation program in adult education using all means of communication.

The programme begins with a group of key people defining the areas of common concern for the town such as education, communication, technology, environment, etc., and these are then examined in depth by various groups within the community. On a basis of their findings it is then possible

101

to organize the month itself. A steering committee needs to appoint an organizer and consultant groups on the main areas of concern. This then leads into the planning of a community-wide assembly which becomes the focal point for the findings of groups and the reactions of people to the issues which have been put before them. It is an intensive means of producing community awareness and involving the church fully in the life of society.

The role of the council of churches in Breadhurst could be to exercise overall control of the whole area and to sort out priorities for the work of the church. It could provide the base for assessment of the various patterns of mission and worship which are being attempted.

II

From this speculative picture we turn to an account of how the churches in fact tackled one New Town. D. H. R. Jones in his very useful book *Planning for Mission*[9] examines the church's role in relation to the planning of New Towns and gives three case studies of how this has in fact proceeded. One of these is Skelmersdale in Lancashire. Skelmersdale was designated as a New Town in 1961 and is planned to have a population of 80,000 by 1980. The major new development between Old Skelmersdale and Up Holland, two old townships, is designed as a single social unit housing 48,000 with no residents being more than twenty minutes' walk from the town centre. At the beginning there were two Anglican parishes, six Methodist chapels, and one church each for the Independent Methodists, Congregationalists, Emmanuel, Pentecostals, Presbyterians and Roman Catholics. By 1970 there were fifteen full-time clergy working there. About a third of those moving in are Roman Catholic. In terms of planning for the area the then Bishop of Warrington took responsibility for Anglican decisions in this matter. This meant that from the Anglican point of view it was comparatively easy for decisions to be made. The Methodists acted through their New Town Commission, though in fact many decisions were made by the Methodist Chairman in consultation with the relevant headquarters' departments.

There was no significant decision-making body in the Presbyterian and Congregational churches. The Roman Catholic church operated through its local parish priests. Dick Jones reports that at no time during the formative period was any thinking done about the nature of the mission of the church in Skelmersdale. This finally emerged when a new group of clergy had moved into the area and a meeting was held between the clergy and the development corporation, only just in time to prevent the churches competing with each other for church sites. The clergy began to meet as a fraternal in 1966 and from this the idea emerged that there should be an ecumenical centre in the middle of the New Town. They drew up plans which suggested a centre which would:

provide a central place of Sunday worship;
provide a centre for the Christian education in worship of the children;
add to the welfare facilities in the town;
provide a church centre for the New Town for pastoral counselling activities;
offer to the town a serious bookshop;
provide a flat or flats for resident clergy, social worker or deaconess.

They made this suggestion to the denominational authorities but none of them replied.

In 1968 a meeting was held at which it was estimated that the project would cost about £85,000. After this some agreement was made about provisional financial commitment from the churches. A further meeting in 1969 went into the legal basis of the project. Then sub-committees were appointed to investigate various aspects of the project. The development corporation was prepared to contribute £10,000 towards the project. The area has been designated as an area of ecumenical experiment, but it is not clear how far the implications of this have been really worked out. An architect has been appointed and the cost of the project is now estimated to be something over £100,000.

Dick Jones, who has analysed this situation carefully is critical of the rather *ad hoc* decision-making procedure which evolved there. He finds it very surprising that there has never been a serious attempt to determine an overall plan for mission in Skelmersdale. He sees danger in the fact that most of the planning has been done by the clergy with very little lay involvement. While the area has been designated as an area of experiment this has been done under Anglican domination and no pattern for reciprocal intercommunion has been worked out. The designation was not worked out on the basis of the BCC document discussed in chapter 4. He wants a much clearer explanation of what the experiment is about though it is clear that the centre will have some experimental aspects. At the moment there is no proper financial commitment involved nor any pattern of common discipline.

Nevertheless progress has been made and out of a pragmatic situation a pragmatic plan has emerged. There is still the need for more policy but it may come in time. Dick Jones concludes with a quotation from one of those closely involved in this project:

It has been almost a full-time job to keep the boat sailing satisfactorily, without raising too many points of principle. We are already bogged down by a good many facts to be sorted and related, and knowing the delicate nature of the whole scheme, some of those who were longer-thinking have had to restrain their enthusiasms to allow the denominational problems to be sorted out. One of the things that is quite clear is that as soon as you raise the idea of ecumenism and you have a set of positive proposals to make, the barriers become even harder between denominations. This is the refuge they retire behind, i.e. anxieties about creating a new denomination, etc.[10]

III

So we have to face the fact that the church is not good at planning. On the whole it is so fragmented that it is virtually impossible to establish an overall strategy. It is very difficult to do so even within one denomination, but when a number are involved it becomes almost impossible. Not only is there no agreement about goals and aims, but the procedures for decision-making within the churches are all totally different and geared to denominational needs. Dick Jones' analysis reveals an alarming insensitivity on behalf of the Anglicans in relation to the other churches. The Methodist Recorder commenting on the BCC report on local councils of churches pointed out that if Methodism wished to be fully involved ecumenically it would have to cut down on its own complex system of structures and organizations. This would be true of every denomination. It is just no use adding ecumenical structures to existing denominational ones. They must take the place of some of them if the churches are really going to act together.

This is a necessary preliminary comment to the examination of a piece of work produced by the industrial chaplains in the diocese of Peterborough. This paper, *Towards a Policy for the Church in an Expanding Society*,[11] was a contribution to the debate in the diocese of Peterborough about the role of the church in the diocese. They begin by facing the need of the church to respond to the rapid population expansion in this country and comment that when the church was faced with the same problem at the time of the Industrial Revolution it responded by building vast numbers of now redundant buildings. What is needed today, they say, is a light, flexible structure for ministry. They then point out, as has already been done in this chapter, that the parochial ministry has become a specialist one and does not relate to the whole of society:

> Parish clergy cater for vital human needs that must be met. They provide essential ministry within the churches' life; but it would be unreasonable to expect them to bear the entire burden of the churches' ministry and attempt to provide for every need expressed by society and the individual.

They introduce the concept of the 'Social Parish' and define it as an area marked out by its distinction as a social entity. Thus education or the social services would be seen as a social parish within which there is a potential ministry to the many people who work within them and are served by them. If society is analysed in this way the church can then begin to ask questions about how it can minister in relation to its manpower and its basic function. They then continue:

> It is usually found that ministers in these social parishes are only acceptable if they are representatives of the whole church. This is because secular authorities fear proliferation of denominational approaches and allegations of partisan treatment. For sound theological as well as these practical reasons the priority to work in unity is clear. Joint planning and consultation with other churches must be normative in establishing this expansion of ministry.

Thus it becomes clear that if the church is to take society seriously it must do so ecumenically. The report then recommends that clergy should be retrained for work in the social parishes but then goes on to point out that the strength of the church in the social parishes lies in the laity who are already there. The clergy will only be there to assist them. They see this as going on alongside the development of group ministries and ecumenical parishes and considerable interchange between them. Their main conclusion is:

> Providing ministry is more important than providing and maintaining plant and cheaper. Ministers for social parishes cost no more

106

than their salaries, housing and expenses and can be given 'on the job' training at low cost. Such ministers are able to spend a large part of their time with the non-church-going 90 per cent of our society and so find themselves, with the laity, continuously at the frontiers of mission and ministry.

They then consider an imaginary situation where the re-deployment of existing clergy, acting on a fully ecumenical basis, would have twenty men working in the domestic ministry and seventeen working in social parishes divided as follows:

Legal/penal	1
Political	1
Health and Welfare	4
Education	4
Industrial	4
Communication	1
Recreational	2

They call for the redeployment and retraining of ministers rather than the establishment of new plant. There can be no doubt that if ecumenical co-operation could be fully established the manpower for this approach would be available.

This is exactly where the uncertainty exists. There seems to be no chance of obtaining such an agreement without organic union and we are aware of all the difficulties which remain before this can be achieved.

We are therefore left with the need for those who have a vision to act upon it and for a new freedom to be expressed in the attitude of many Christians. Whether we are looking at a specific situation or at a whole regional approach the need for a new attitude is equally apparent. Without it there can be little future for the church today. It requires a new open-ness, a new acceptance of each other, an appreciation of the centrality of diversity and a new theological understanding. Much of this is summed up in the theological statement with which the Peterborough chaplains close their paper:

In Christ God has become man.

In Him the Divine and the Human are one.

In Him manhood was taken into God.

In Christ God came to us – so closely and integrally that the divine and human could not be separated out.

Hence his name EMMANUEL God with us.

With Christ began a new era in human history.

Before Christ came, man was indeed already the crown of creation, the spearhead of evolution. But he was still lower than the angels.

Christ was the New Man.

Christ was the first fruits of redeemed humanity.

Men in Christ are, in their turn, New Men,

Members of the New Creation,

Citizens of the Heavenly City,

Travelling towards their home in the New Jerusalem.

Since Christ, the world is no longer excluded from holiness.

Christ, in His flesh, rent the veil of the Temple.

The sacred and profane are no longer separated.

Just as manhood was, in Christ, taken into God, so in the redeemed humanity, the rest of creation can follow.

Its groaning and travailing can be swallowed up in joy,

Its stones can be foundations for the Holy City,

Its waters can sustain the Tree of Life given for the healing of the nations.

This is the Good News for the people who walk in darkness.

This is the Gospel.

This is the background against which we must view the Church.

The Church is ONE because God is One.

The Church is HOLY because it is called by God.

The Church is CATHOLIC because all nations shall bring their glory into it.

The Church is APOSTOLIC because God has sent it out with tasks to perform.

The 'true' Church is that portion of mankind which responds to the grace of God, in worship and love.

Historic 'churches' are those bodies of men which consciously aim to respond.

The whole Church is laity. The laity is the whole Church.

The clergy are those within the laity who equip the rest for ministry which is the work of the whole Church.

There are differences of administration, but the same Lord.

There is diversity of function, but only one Church.

The life of the Church is not in its structure, but its structure either upholds or restricts its life.

108

NOTES

1. E. P. Thompson, *The Making of the English Working Class*, Penguin 1968, pp.45, 50.

2. T. Rennie Warburton, 'The Faith Mission: a Study in Inter-denominationalism', in D. Martin (ed.), *A Sociological Yearbook of Religion in Britain 2*, SCM Press 1969, pp.75–102.

3. *Keeping Pace With Tomorrow*, issued by the General Assembly of the Church of Scotland 1971.

4. G. Reid, *The Gagging of God*, Hodder & Stoughton 1969.

5. L. Newbigin, *Honest Religion for Secular Man*, SCM Press 1967, pp.105f.

6. M. Wilson, *The Hospital – a Place of Truth*, Institute for the Study of Worship and Religious Architecture, Birmingham University 1971.

7. *Maidstone – a Closer Look*, Maidstone Council of Churches 1965.

8. Louis Wilson, *Town Talk Manual*, Project People Toronto 1968.

9. D. H. R. Jones, *Planning for Mission. A Study of Church Decision-Making in New Towns*, New Town Ministers' Association 1971, available from The Pastoral Centre, High Street, Dawley, Telford, Shropshire, price £1·20.

10. *Op. cit.*, p.63.

11. *Towards a Policy for the Church in an Expanding Society*, issued by the Industrial Chaplains of the Peterborough Diocese, 1969.

7   The Emerging Church

I

On the site of the old Croydon Airport, a place of much
pioneering in the days of early flying, there is being established a new housing estate called Roundshaw. The population of the area is about 5,500 and will be 8,000 when the
project is completed. It is not a large development and the
provision of amenities in terms of shops, social services and
schools has so far been quite small. This is partly due to its
proximity to Croydon, which is a main shopping centre. In
1967 Derek Jones, an Anglican priest, moved into a council
flat on the estate at the same time as the first residents. He
worked there alone for the first two and a half years of the
experiment, though he was acting on behalf of all the
churches. In 1970 he was joined by a Congregational
minister, Keith Spence. The work of the church in Roundshaw begun by Derek Jones consisted of visiting all the people
as they arrived. He was usually the first person they met and
therefore the person who provided them with the local
information which they needed. From these initial contacts
two things followed. One was the formation of a Tenants'
Association of which Derek Jones was the first secretary.
The other was the establishment of a local newspaper, the
Roundshaw Courier, which has become the chief organ of
communication in Roundshaw. From the very beginning a
deliberate decision was taken not to put up a church building
in Roundshaw. Early on a pattern of worship emerged for

110

the experiment, and this has remained the same ever since. Derek Jones has described this as follows:

> ... practising Christians met in somebody's living room, normally spent an hour discussing either some aspect of the life of Roundshaw which was in somebody's mind or the nature of the experiment itself, following this up with an informal celebration of the holy communion.

The clergy have established themselves within the development of community life. Derek Jones has been appointed community organizer by the Tenants' Association and in this capacity he has more than once come into conflict with the local authorities on behalf of the residents. The early days of Roundshaw when everyone knew everyone else are now past, and for many it is just the place where they happen to live and they have little interest in what is going on there. There also seems to be a high proportion of people with personal problems which require special community care.

The *Roundshaw Courier* began in the early days of the experiment as a community paper to exchange news and information. Derek Jones described its functions as follows:

> It has helped to create a sense of Roundshaw's identity.
> It communicates information on all official decisions in a readable form.
> It helps Roundshaw people to talk to one another.
> It tries to go deep enough to mirror a living neighbourhood.
> It gives individuals and groups a voice.
> It is able to comment, often in highly critical terms, on establishment attitudes and decisions.
> It can act as interpreter of social change.

As Roundshaw has developed other means of communication have evolved in the area. There are many places where people now meet and talk (shop, youth centre, doctor's surgery, etc.). Public meetings are not as popular as they used to be, but there has been a growth of special interest groups and informal discussions. Derek Jones thinks that the experimental church may be seen as one of these discussion groups, though this should not be the church's sole expression. Social events also seem to be important in helping people to meet each other in a new community.

The clergy are convinced that visiting must continue to be a main function of the experiment. They describe three types of visiting which he sees as important in the area:

(a) *In connection with Courier stories.* Usually, this is an attempt to get a person to communicate with us about his problem, his views, his interests, etc. We go to considerable trouble to uncover why a person feels in a particular way, why he engages in a particular interest, etc. If we are doing a story of estate-wide interest, we make sure our interviewees are from as many different parts of Roundshaw as possible.

(b) *House to house.* This has, so far, been more possible for Derek than for Keith, who would like to do more of it when time allows. We take a particular area and visit all houses. This enable us to complete a 'profile' of the area and vastly increases our knowledge of how Roundshaw is thinking. Conversation is not, of course, limited to Roundshaw affairs, and we take trouble to elicit views of work, politics, leisure, etc. Even religion is sometimes raised!

(c) *Families with problems.* There has recently been a big increase in this field, both of us having to spend considerable time with particular families. We are co-operating where possible with social workers, health visitors, the doctor, etc.

Visiting we conclude, is a vitally important part of establishing and sustaining the relationship between the experiment and the estate. When people relate that they feel 'comfortable' with us, we feel that we have communicated a concern for them, without strings – people do not think of us as a recruiting agency.

The *Roundshaw Courier* has an editorial group of eight reporters which meets once a month to review what is happening in Roundshaw. This group is clearly a main ingredient in the work of the church. Here the moral and political implications of life in Roundshaw come to the surface. The *Courier* tries to help people talk to each other. It is not just concerned with news but with the reasons and attitudes behind it. It is the only paper some people in Roundshaw read. It has a strong editorial policy which itself expresses quite a lot of the Christian gospel. Derek Jones has expressed its main thesis in the following terms:

(a) Everybody has something to contribute to the life of the community. Many have been conditioned by our social system to believe that they have no talents; this assumption must be contradicted and proved wrong.

(b) Our social system has also conditioned people to expect too little from life. Everybody has the right to communal and individual fulfilment. This condition may be attained – and people must work at it, despite many discouragements from those who hold power.

(c) People have the right and the responsibility to shape their own destiny.

(d) People are alienated from the centres of power, which, as they become bigger, also become more impersonal. Reconciliation is impossible unless those who hold power and influence come out of their offices, listen to people, think of them as persons not things.

(e) In our society the economic cost is regularly put before social cost. This order must be reversed.

(f) Whilst individual responsibility for social ills cannot be disregarded, the causes often lie embedded in society's many remaining injustices; remove the structural injustices, and individuals will respond with renewed confidence.

(g) English society, with its well-known propensity towards class stratification, accords a low status to 'council tenants'. Whole groups of people cannot be summed up in this way; mutuality between people of different backgrounds is possible and desirable once it is recognized that there are differences, but these differences can be combined to create a healthy whole.

It is not surprising that the Roundshaw experiment has a strong political emphasis in its work. In relation to the church, the people there are involved in an ongoing debate on the relation of proclamation and service and what could be defined as specifically 'Christian' about the experiment. Many people have a concept of the church as a place you go to for sacraments and services. The Roundshaw experiment is trying to communicate that the church is people living and working out the gospel in their whole lives. Therefore many people do not quite understand what is going on and this reversal of ideas cannot be accepted easily by all of them. There is little doubt that present Christian language and ideas are not communicating to people today. It is good to try and find language which does do so. Whether it will succeed or not will not be known for some time. It makes it all the more important that the experiment has a proper process of evaluation for what is going on. A consultative group has been set up to help the experiment assess what it is doing. But this evaluation must itself be carefully worked out, as Derek Jones comments:

> The criterion for success in the Roundshaw experiment is not 'How many people have decided to join the church and attend church worship as a result of our activities?' but rather 'What is the quality of the relationship between the church and the community – and is the church making an effective contribution to neighbourhood life, making a difference to the quality of its life?'
> ... Provisionally it could be said that the experiment is widely trusted as a body which cares about the community and that many more of the ordinary non-church-going public are in relationship with us than is normal. We could not claim, nor should we declare, monolithic support. There is, on the contrary, a good deal of confusion about what the experiment is up to – this we encourage because it demonstrates that the experiment is the provoking thought.

Roundshaw is still growing; the next few years will be crucial in its development but we can already learn a few tentative lessons from what has been going on.

When an experiment of this type takes place the lines between church and society become very blurred. This will be regarded with great alarm by some but will be welcomed by others. Those who see the church as a place where people can find their identity and purpose may see this as a threat. On the other hand, if the mission of the church is seen in terms of co-operation with the mission of God in the whole of society, then it is very important that the edges are blurred. It becomes the means by which mission is possible.

Secondly, we see the church expressing itself not as a

114

building but as a means of communication within the community. The church is of course always communicating what it is by what it does and this may be one reason why modern man finds so much of the church uninteresting and unhelpful. By deliberately concentrating on enabling people to communicate with each other, through meetings, visiting and the *Roundshaw Courier*, the church is seen more clearly to have an enabling role within society and one which is geared to improve the quality of life.

Another aspect of this is that the traditional denominational differences seem to disappear altogether. When the church takes the structures of society seriously the denominational divisions become meaningless and cannot be sustained. The gospel, and not allegiance to any particular Christian community, becomes the point of unity.

This is a serious attempt to relate to a total community and to community life. Personal and family life is not ignored, but it is put in the wider social context which moulds so much of it anyhow. The main thrust of the experiment is not to resolve the divisions of the church directly but to find new patterns of mission and ministry which may in the process put the problem of Christian division into a new perspective.

Paul Tillich,[1] writing after the Second World War, prophesied that in the post-war world there would be a great threat to individual identity and a loss of community. He saw the need for what he called 'anonymous and esoteric groups' which would include religious people together with others. Their function would be to resist the trends towards depersonalization and to fight for community and personality. They would be able to do this, he said, because they would consist of people who knew the ultimate meaning of life even if they could not express it. He called on the democratic governments to protect these groups against

115

political or economic suppression so that their creativity could help to produce a new social pattern.

Roundshaw may be an example of what he had in mind. The church should give it support and protection to allow it and other experiments to continue.

II

The stories in this book demonstrate the interaction of mission and unity on each other. Groups of Christians in many places are seeking new modes of expression for their commitment to the Christian gospel. Some are within the formal church, others are outside it. They are diverse in expression but they have some things in common. They express a willingness to experiment and a responsible freedom which is not shown in other parts of church life. These are not success stories, they are not completed stories either. This analysis is essentially an interim one but may help us to make some tentative conclusions about the emerging shape of the church.

Reference has been made several times in this book to the Nottingham Faith and Order Conference. That conference represented a height of optimism in the churches about ecumenical growth in Britain. The call to the churches to covenant together for unity by 1980 was a serious call which several churches were willing to accept. The Church of England did not see its way to accept the concept of covenant and, while the subsequent debate made allowance for the existing union schemes, the efforts of the churches in England were mainly centred on the union schemes between Anglicans and Methodists and between Presbyterians and Congregationalists. In Wales the situation is somewhat different and there the work on a scheme of covenanting continues. The long-drawn-out nature of the Presbyterian–Congregational conversations and the way in which the

116

Church of England 'turned down the invitation which it itself made to the Methodists' (Gordon Rupp's phrase) have led to considerable disillusion among many about the possibilities of achieving organic unity in England. The Presbyterians and Congregationalists are now on the way to becoming a united church, but until an episcopal church achieves union with a non-episcopal church these doubts will remain.

It should be clear from these pages that nothing short of organic union will do. To attempt union only from the bottom up is to limit one's concept of mission solely to the residential and parochial area of life. One of the values of ecumenical experiments is that they enable the denominations to test out various patterns without having to commit themselves to any one in advance. Ecumenical experiment is a valuable complement to schemes for organic union. The church must have a very careful strategy and considerable overall planning. The main factor which militates against this is the division of the churches. An overall strategy for mission can only come from a united church. It is false to think that this is the kind of planning that the churches can do through the British Council of Churches. That council is a forum for common action and consultation – it cannot co-ordinate the work of the churches. Short of organic union the churches will have to organize their own life and activities and this is bound to take precedence over everything else. While the denominations may be able to participate in some local experiment they could not reorganize themselves for total ecumenical action short of organic union. Also we have seen in chapter 5 that one intractable problem is that of church membership. People who join the church for the first time in an ecumenical parish have to join one of the existing denominations as well. This problem can only be resolved when there is one church.

It may well be that the real disillusionment over unity has come from people having far too static a view of unity. There is a great diversity of expression of the church emerging today. There has always been a diversity of expression within the church, but it has not been recognized as something creative and revealing the essential nature of unity. Christian tradition has laid emphasis on the divisive nature of sin and has seen unity as an expression of men's unity with God and with one another. This is a valid emphasis but it needs to be balanced by an awareness of the fundamental diversity of man given in creation. God's redemption is not to be a denial of his creation. What men bring to their unity is essentially their diversity and their uniqueness as God's individual creatures. Unity should help to promote this diversity and not to deny it.

This diversity in the expression of the church was one of the main findings of the World Council of Churches' depth studies of fifteen churches in various parts of the world. The analysis of this study entitled 'World Studies of Churches in Mission' revealed that while all the churches which they examined were identifiably the church, there was very little which they really had in common. The churches all seemed to move on a scale between almost complete identification with society and complete isolation from it. What this shows is how far the churches are conditioned by the culture in which they are placed. That culture will reflect itself in the church and depending upon its own attitude the church will either feel able to be related to the society or will feel antagonized and preserve its identity over against society.

The group appointed by the WCC to examine the fifteen reports came to the conclusion that they must affirm diversity as an essential mark of the church.

Some may be hesitant to acknowledge as part of the church, One, Holy, Catholic and Apostolic, groups of Christians as are some of these, with a rudimentary knowledge of Christian teaching, with apparent gaps in their Christian commitment, with strange and unfamiliar forms of worship and with doctrinal emphases which may be thought unscriptural. And yet in spite of these differences, all of them confess in their own way that they belong to the church of Jesus Christ. This is clearly beyond dispute and it is on this basis that we affirm 'this is the church . . . in its *diversity*'.[2]

They affirm that this diversity goes deep and provides some of the richness of ecumenical encounter. This diversity can also be seen in churches of the same tradition. So the Anglican churches in Birmingham, Buganda and the Solomon Islands have very little in common. Churches from the same geographical area can be extremely diverse. Diversity is as essential for the church as it is for individuals. As the church grows in its own self-awareness it develops an identity of its own and diversity becomes part of its own life.

The other side of an acceptance of this diversity is a willingness to accept others as equal within the church. The general tendency of church union schemes has not laid emphasis on this. They have laid great emphasis on the form of church government which will bring together the polity of the participating churches. Inevitably this relates to the polity of the past, not of the present. Hence diversity does not take much part in it. The one exception to this is the Plan of Union of the Consultation on Church Union in the USA. They say that the scheme allows for diversity and flexibility:

We seek not to diminish freedom under the gospel but to enhance it. Some authoritative structures are necessary but under Christ's Lordship every appropriate channel of responsible freedom in decision-making should be left open. Our concern is for the church and its mission. It must not be immobilized by a majority which ignores or otherwise coerces a minority, nor by a minority which is divisive and finally obstructs conscientious action.[3]

Is this enough? Certainly to construct a united church which will allow for freedom and diversity will be a very delicate business and will need to be kept under constant review.

We need a much stronger and more dynamic concept of unity. The key to this has already been provided by Ernst Käsemann in his commentary on John 17. With his great emphasis on the gospel as freedom, Käsemann gives a definition which allows the maximum amount of freedom:

> Unity does not mean uniformity, but solidarity, the tension-filled interconnection between those who differ among themselves. Christian unity implies the freedom of the individual in the exercise of the gift of freedom and of the service entrusted to him. Thus it teaches men to tolerate and even to appreciate tensions, to avoid pressing everything into the same mould. This solidarity advocates freedom to the very limits of what would break up the fellowship. If it were otherwise, Christianity would become sterile and unfit for service.[4]

Here is the unity which we should be seeking, a unity which welcomes diversity and freedom and accepts others in Christ. Such a unity would encourage an experimental style of Christianity, which will enable Christians to find new expressions of life without the threat of schism or excommunication.

Lewis Mudge in his book *The Crumbling Walls* has examined experiments in eucharistic practice in the churches. He looks at some places and occasions where the present eucharistic discipline of Roman Catholics and others have been ignored. This leads him to call for an experimental polity for the church.

> The Christian ministry [is] from freedom to freedom, from risk to risk. If such a ministry is to be credible, it must have both its social and its symbolic location fully within the ambiguous human situations to which it intrinsically speaks.

He then goes on to define the type of church which he sees emerging. This kind of church

> would have to reflect the main features of the new Christian communities; their contextual nature, their adaptability, their independence of concentrations of power and wealth. It would, on the other hand, have to find ways of keeping the tradition of biblical faith from

distortion and of producing theological reflection on the faith adequate to its mission. None of these requirements, in the light of past experience, should be taken lightly.[5]

The models given in this book would substantiate this opinion. We should not forget the requirement given here to preserve the biblical tradition from distortion. This must be done, but it will not be easy. In the past ecumenical thinking has sought to do this by establishing certain basic statements of faith which must be accepted. The Lambeth Quadrilateral which laid down for Anglicans the Bible, the creeds, the apostolic ministry and the dominical sacraments as the basis of unity, was an attempt to do that. This cannot be enough in itself. The way in which the Lambeth Quadrilateral is interpreted is changing greatly, not least in the interpretation given to it by the last Lambeth Conference. The application of these principles could well express itself in very diverse ways. Moreover there is a growing awareness among theologians that the scriptures themselves as well as the traditional Christian doctrines are so culturally conditioned that it is not easy, some would say impossible, to extract a core of truth which will be fully meaningful for us today. We can only explore this way in faith. So far church union negotiations have not taken the findings of current theological thinking seriously enough. They seem to operate much more in terms of historical theology. Hence church union comes to be seen as a rather nostalgic historical activity. We need a much more dynamic view of the church which does its own theology as it acts in mission in the world. Thus Lewis Mudge sees a new type of church emerging more or less in spite of the present church. Experimental communities will have to emerge in loyal opposition to existing church structures. This new type of Christian gathering

will be much more mobile, much more willing to see the church in temporary encounters. It will replace channels of authority with

121

channels of communication. It will be highly decentralized except at moments when the situation calls for united witness.[6]

We catch here echoes of the Roundshaw experiment. The concept of the church as a channel of communication is important but the fact that Roundshaw is being supported by the churches and not in opposition to it gives us hope that the churches are beginning to see the point of making experiments. It is to be hoped that there will never be one single pattern.

Church union schemes have also assumed that we know what the church is and that all we have to do is to put the pieces of divided Christendom together. This is to ignore the fact that the church is a mystery which we are all trying to discover and enter into. We are all making a common exploration to discover the church. If Gerald Downing[7] is right it is as impossible for us to discover the historical church as it is to discover the historical Christ. In that case it is not necessary for us to carry on fighting the battles of the past in relation to baptism, the creeds or church order, but to try and discover the shape for the church which we need today. It is false to talk about reunion, we need rather to consider what T. O. Wedel called 'the Coming Great Church'. In considering this we need to look not to the past but to the future. Thus Schlink calls us to think of unity within the dimension of the Coming Christ.[8] Viewed from this dimension our divisions become meaningless. We see the interim nature of the church itself and we become less concerned to preserve existing structures because the Coming Christ brings his fullness with him.

It was Dietrich Bonhoeffer[9] who reminded us not to confuse the ultimate and the penultimate. One of the main problems for the church is that it has treated itself as ultimate instead of seeing itself as an interim body which exists to serve God and his Kingdom. We shall only be alarmed at experimentation if we think that there is something ultimate and God-given about church buildings, church government or church order. These are not ultimate concerns and they must not be allowed to become so. God alone is our ultimate concern. If we saw this clearly we could move to unity more easily because the things which divide us would not seem so important to us.

III

If this is our vision of the type of unity we seek, how can we move from where we are towards this? This book has been concerned to show new patterns and to describe people's attempts to discover a new unity in mission. Another book could be written to show what a powerless state the church appears to be in today. All denominations are reporting declining membership, the surveys of church activities in various areas reveal a gloomy picture. The whole problem of the dominant/dependent clergy/laity relationship is one of the main reasons why there is so little change in the church. The church is certainly meeting people's needs, but it may well be meeting their need to dominate and be dependent rather than leading them to responsible freedom. It is only too easy to present a very gloomy picture of the church today, but it would not be the whole picture. While much is wrong the church still has great resources in money and manpower. It can still gather together more people than almost any other organization in Britain. It exercises a serving ministry in many places, and is a support to many people. There is considerable interest in Christianity, though not so much interest in institutional religion in this country. The opportunities for the communication of the gospel have never been better, but is the church able to take them?

Following the showing of a film about the Church of England on the BBC Programme 'Panorama' in May 1971, a correspondence in *The Times* included a letter from the Bishop of Stepney which contained the following paragraphs:

Who is to say, where failure and success really lie? Is a church full every Sunday with middle-class suburbia more or less successful than a working-class parish where pews are pretty empty but where 'unseen but not unknown', Christian 'community' is coming to life again in small groups and house meetings? Is the only sign of the power of the Holy Spirit at work in our great cities supposed to be vast numbers at worship once a week in vast buildings supported by vast endowments?

With every day I spend in Stepney I grow more hopeful, not less, about the future of Christianity here. I know, as BBC commentators cannot know, the 'growing points' both within and without the parochial structures, which indicate unmistakably the power of the Spirit of God. I am prepared to state unequivocally that the very problems confronting the church in East London (and humanly speaking they are tremendous) are the conditions of its renewal and are seen as such by all committed Christians in these parts.

For God's sake, let us 'seethe with anger' not against the BBC but against our own mistaken idolatries of status, buildings and popularity.[10]

These words could well be the conclusion to this book, but if they are justified, perhaps it is possible to begin a list of those things which will enable the churches to take advantage of these growing points.

1. *The value of small groups.* Small groups meeting together for prayer, study or action can well be the spearhead of united mission. What many people who have seen this much have not seen is that the small group can be a sufficient expression of the church in itself. It is not a second best to church attendance; it is church attendance of a new sort. At the same time the danger of introversion must be faced and the need for groups to be in touch with others, to change membership, and to identify with the wider church is also important. We gain a new insight into the nature of *episcope* if we see one of the roles of the ministry as co-ordinating the work of many groups. This must be a personal job – it

124

cannot be done by a committee and perhaps points to a new type of bishop in the church.

2. *The need for loyal rebellion.* Change may well come out of the tension between the *status quo* and those who wish to change it. The willingness of some to create 'illegal facts' and to work for an alternative church may be just the impetus which is needed to move the institution on further. Those who do this should not go outside the institution but should realize their freedom within it. There is no need to ask someone's permission to do something new. All that is needed is the will and the freedom to do it. The dynamics of change work more effectively in this way than if an outright revolution is attempted

3. *The need for a mission-oriented theology.* Such a theology sees the church not as an end in itself but as a means of serving the mission of God. It requires that we take seriously not only individuals but the whole structure of society. Such a theology enables us to think of the flexible nature of mission and the church and thus not try to press everything into one mould. This is much more related to the facts of life than many other theologies. It requires an experimental approach to theology and to church structures, and may well require political activity in society.

4. *The need for an overall strategy.* The massive resources of the church are not to be deplored or disposed of easily. They are to be geared for mission. Therefore much more emphasis needs to be given to training in mission and to relating to the social structures. Some places have found that they can do this only if resources of money and manpower are set free. There can be no overall planning unless we become one church.

5. *A new spirituality.* There will be no change, no unity and no mission unless people want it. At the heart of the ecumenical problem lies the spiritual problem of helping

people to use their freedom in Christ creatively. To achieve this Christians must first rid themselves of their fear of failure. Christians spend a lot of time justifying themselves when they are supposed to let themselves be justified by Christ. Failure is what we witness and confess in the crucifixion of Christ. It lies at the heart of our faith. If we were prepared to risk failure we might see some new successes. If like Christ the church was prepared to die, then it might begin to live. If Christians were prepared to accept their justification by Christ and live in his freedom then new life would soon appear. This needs a new attitude of mind – a new conversion.

Ian Suttie, in his book *The Origins of Love and Hate*, says that there are two types of Christian, the Augustinian and the Hellenistic:

> The Hellenistic transmitters of Christianity conceived that they had something so good that it was their duty to share it; the Augustinian felt that to save his own soul he had to conquer others for God . . . [The Hellenistic approach] conceived of man as the potential ally of God rather than the innate and irreconcilable rebel against him. Its conception of religious life might be represented thus – 'God and man versus evil' whereas Augustine's was 'God versus man and evil'.[11]

The Hellenist accepted the world and dedicated it to God; the Augustinian wanted to make everyone like himself. The one expressed confidence in God and therefore acceptance of the world. The other, uncertain about himself, and therefore anxious, needed to be surrounded by the likeminded. This is not the place to go into the rights or wrongs of Suttie's interpretation. These two attitudes do exist. For Christian unity and for Christian mission the Hellenistic approach is the one that must be cultivated. It is as we are prepared to accept others in Christ without a desire to make them conform that a unity in diversity can be expressed. The power of acceptance to change others is far greater than the power of compulsion or pressure of any sort. Herein lies our basic need. We can only be free and accepting Christians because Christ freely accepts us. It is those who, in however limited a way, have found this freedom, who are able to experiment in mission and progress in unity. This is the heart of the ecumenical problem and the inspiration of ecumenical action.

NOTES

1. P. Tillich, *The Protestant Era*, Nisbet 1951, p.295.
2. S. G. Mackie (ed.), *Can the Churches be Compared?*, WCC 1970, p.88.
3. *Plan of Union*, Consultation on Church Union, USA, 1970, pp.12–13.
4. E. Käsemann, *The Testament of Jesus*, SCM Press 1968, p.56.
5. L. Mudge, *The Crumbling Walls*, Westminster Press, USA, 1970, pp.158–9.
6. *Ibid.*, p.164.
7. F. G. Downing, *The Church and Jesus*, SCM Press 1968.
8. E. Schlink, *The Coming Christ and the Coming Church*, Oliver & Boyd 1968.
9. D. Bonhoeffer, *Ethics*, SCM Press 1955.
10. Letter to *The Times*, 28 May 1971.
11. I. Suttie, *The Origins of Love and Hate*, Penguin Books 1963, p.142.

Epilogue

These are just a few stories of the way in which mission in unity is being sought today. This is not in any way an exhaustive or complete list, and readers will all be able to add stories of their own. This is the way the church grows and changes through Christians making and telling stories for themselves. But this requires freedom – a freedom which only Christ can bring and which is exercised responsibly. Responsible freedom is the essence of story-telling and story-making. So we may send out signals of new life and new hope to others.

It is hoped that this book will encourage others to find the freedom to make stories for themselves and to tell them to others. This is the way the church is made new and Christians are made one.